Martin R Gillott

CONFESSIONS OF A WRESTLER

The Autobiography of
British Wrestling Legend
Jackie 'Glitterboy' Evans

Martin R Gillott

CONFESSIONS OF A WRESTLER

The Autobiography of
British Wrestling Legend
Jackie 'Glitterboy' Evans

MEREO
Cirencester

Mereo Books

1A The Wool Market Dyer Street Cirencester Gloucestershire GL7 2PR
An imprint of Memoirs Publishing www.mereobooks.com

Confessions of a Wrestler: 978-1-86151-067-9

First published in Great Britain in 2014
by Mereo Books, an imprint of Memoirs Publishing

The address for Memoirs Publishing Group Limited can be found at
www.memoirspublishing.com

The Memoirs Publishing Group Ltd Reg. No. 7834348

The Memoirs Publishing Group supports both The Forest Stewardship Council® (FSC®) and
the PEFC® leading international forest-certification organisations. Our books carrying both the
FSC label and the PEFC® and are printed on FSC®-certified paper. FSC® is the only
forest-certification scheme supported by the leading environmental organisations including
Greenpeace. Our paper procurement policy can be found at
www.memoirspublishing.com/environment

Typeset in 11.5/16pt Plantin
by Wiltshire Associates Publisher Services Ltd. Printed and bound in Great Britain by
Printondemand-Worldwide, Peterborough PE2 6XD

The lady in the front row

Why do you really hate me
As I strut around the ring
And start to hurl abuse at me
When I haven't done a thing?
I'm here to entertain you
And to win a bout or two
It doesn't help me, not one bit
When you spit and hiss and boo.
You are such a dear old lady
Of that I have no doubt
But when I'm on the canvas
You treat me like a lout!
I'm just a harmless wrestler
Trying hard to earn a crust
You stub your fag out on my back
And try my head to bust
Take that brick out from your handbag
Sit back and take a rest
Enjoy the show for what it is
And let me do my best.
We are both human beings
When all is said and done
After all, you are my mother
And I am still your son.

Martin R Gillott

Contents

Dedication
Acknowledgements
Foreword, by T P Bayliss
Introduction

I dedicate this book to Ruth, my lovely wife, best friend and soulmate, who has always been there for me, without question.

Acknowledgements

I would like to thank all my family, friends and fellow wrestlers for their support in the writing of this book and their patience, understanding and help in reminding me of one or two stories that had momentarily slipped my mind. Those that I live with, those I have worked with and one or two of you who I have got drunk with, I dedicate this all to you, as without you, there would have been no memories.

I also dedicate this to my good friends Karen and Glyn Lindley. Karen, who was good enough to cast an eye over my work and prevented me from showing my grammatical ignorance, and Glyn, who over the years listened to my countless tales from the past without flinching or yawning.

To my good friend Lyn Cinderey, whose advice is always of value, and always taken.

And last but not least, to my darling wife Ruth, to whom I owe so much and who never once lost her temper with me as I crashed my blunderous way through her best laptop.

Foreword

I first met Martin Gillott, aka Jackie 'Glitterboy' Evans, in 1970 when he was beginning to make a name for himself in the world of wrestling. He was proving himself with a host of different promoters and I was a humble Master Of Ceremonies, announcing a variety of wrestlers as they entered the ring. The following years would show his rise in the game whilst I myself could only manage to reach the height of referee.

It was on our first meeting in his home town of Stroud that I very soon realised that Martin was a person who took his sport seriously and lived for his art. I followed his progress over the coming years but was never surprised at the way he worked himself hard enough to eventually reach the top. We lost touch over the years, although I managed to follow his career through several press cuttings and issues of Ringsport magazine, which readily available at that time, and as luck would have it, we met up again shortly before he finally hung up his boots.

I have been privileged to know many of the wrestlers throughout my life, but I don't think that there was a more dedicated and workmanlike person in or out of the ring. He still retains that rare ability to take an awkward situation and make light of it, putting people at their ease and finding a suitable solution that suits everyone involved. This is undoubtedly a gift that few people have, and Martin had it by the bucketful. He cared about people in his company and would always help in any way possible. He would recall his wrestling days with great fondness, as you will no doubt agree, once you have read this book. As I read it, I can still hear him telling me some of the antics that he got up to over the years.

The only thing missing from the print is that little chuckle from time to time as Martin relayed some anecdote from his bygone days that still means a lot to him. I am proud to say that I lived some of his early stories alongside him and will always be proud to call him a dear friend.

T P Bayliss

Introduction

I was twelve years old when I first knew I wanted to be a wrestler, and it made my school life difficult. All my mates wanted to be footballers or train drivers, but not me. I must have driven them all mad, as wrestling was the only thing I could talk about. As far as I know anoraks hadn't been invented then, so I guess I would have been called a "duffle coat."

My PE teacher had the right idea when confronted with my reluctance to play football. He took me one side and mentioned that if I wanted to become a wrestler, then what better training could there be than to be in goal? After all, there would be plenty of opportunity to throw myself on the ground, which was something I was going to have to master if I was to have a life in the ring. He won me over and from that day, I could always be relied on to be in goal. That was until I went to secondary school, when I lost that crown to a lad called Steven Banyard, who was a lot taller than me and could keep the high balls out from the back of the net. That was the demise of my footballing days.

I tried my hand at other sports but it was no good, it was wrestling or nothing. What I hadn't realised was that being in the ring was a fraction of the life that I had chosen. The rest was taken up with copious amounts of travelling and living out of a suitcase for sometimes weeks on end, and of course, having a very limited social life.

Now that I can look back on it, was it all worth it? Of course it was, and if I had my time over, I would do it all again.

Martin R Gillott
aka Jackie 'Glitterboy' Evans

A childhood passion

It was one Friday evening in summer. I was about twelve years old at the time and I was running for all I was worth to get home as quickly as possible. After all, I doubt whether any other twelve-year-old was the keeper of such important information, and it needed to be relayed at the first possible moment. As I ran around the last corner, before reaching home, I wondered how best to frame the news to my family. So important was it that I didn't have time to shut the garden gate. That would have to be done later. I knew how much Dad hated the gate left open, but this was ground-breaking news.

I rushed into the hallway of our home and shouted to my elder brother as I kicked off my shoes, "Dad, Dad! Where's Dad?" I did not have time to wait for an answer.

"He's in the living room" came the shouted reply. I rushed past breathless but still in high excitement. "I've just been up the shop and there's a poster" I said. My father aroused himself from a quick nap. "What are you going on about boy? Sit down and get your breath back, then tell me what all the panic is about."

"It's a wrestling poster on the wall outside the shop, Dad. Wrestling, like we see on the telly. It's coming here in three weeks' time. Can we go, Dad?"

Mother entered, followed by my three brothers, to see what all the fuss was about and I quickly but breathlessly relayed my very important news to all.

Ever since I could remember I had spent a couple of hours every Saturday afternoon sitting cross-legged on the floor while we as a family took part in that well known ritual of being glued to the television from four o'clock onwards watching World of Sport and in particular the wrestling. It wasn't only our family; people all over Great Britain were doing the same. It was the one time of the week that could be guaranteed to find us all in the same room at the same time, watching the same programme.

"It's coming here Mum, to the Subscription Rooms in Stroud. Can we go? Please say yes". After a few words exchanged with Dad, Mum agreed, so I was dispatched back up to the shop with a paper and pencil to write down all the details needed in order to purchase our tickets. I guarded this bit of paper with my life, as I retraced my steps back home, although, at a somewhat slower pace.

"Someone will have to catch the bus into Stroud and get the tickets," Dad said. Like a lot of families in those days, we never owned a car. It was agreed that Mum would get them when she was next in town.

Within a few days we were the proud owners of four tickets. When I enquired why only four, I was informed that my younger brother Alan was just a little bit too young to be going and that Dad would stay home and look after him. After all, said Dad, "I'm happy just watching it on the telly. You all go with your Mum and enjoy yourselves".

That three weeks seemed to take forever to go by, and in the meantime, between carefully scrutinizing the tickets on the mantelpiece and studying the poster outside the village shop, I had learned off by heart the names of all the wrestlers, who they were fighting and indeed where they were from. Nearly five decades have passed since then but I still remember one or two of them. There was Big Chief Thunderbird vs Bronco Jack Cassidy. Then Reg Yates vs Jim Moser. OK, maybe it wasn't Les Kellett or Jackie Pallo but it was still wrestling. For three whole weeks, I would read that poster on my way home from school.

I remember the day of the wrestling, well. It was the same day I was told off at school for not concentrating, but how could I when there was such an important event as wrestling to think about? I couldn't talk to my school chums about it; they were busy talking about football. How football could possibly be of more interest than wrestling, I didn't understand.

I couldn't get home quick enough, and much to the amusement of my family, I was ready to go at 4.30 pm. "It's half past four," said Mum. "The bus doesn't come until a quarter to seven, we haven't had tea yet." How could I think of food at a time like this? Of course, I did manage to eat my meal and spent the rest of the time pacing up and down the hallway.

"Is it still there?" said Dad. I stopped pacing. "Is what still there?" I answered.

"The front door. You must have checked it a dozen times in the last half an hour."

Eventually we were on our way to the bus stop and at last, my big adventure had started. We arrived in plenty of time and I was overwhelmed by the number of people that such a small venue could hold. With my eyes wide open, I was glued to the huge ring in the middle of the room - and how near we were sitting to the action. The whole thing seemed like a fantastic dream, but a lot bigger than I was expecting. What's more, it was in colour.

We took our seats and, as always, Dad had done us proud. Right in the front row, where we wouldn't miss a thing. As the hall filled up, the Master Of Ceremonies entered the ring and made the first announcements over the microphone. Within a few minutes, the first two wrestlers entered the ring. My goodness! If I were ever going to stand a chance of being a wrestler, I would have to get a lot bigger than I was. I was only twelve but even at that tender age, I knew that I would have to get a spurt on, get a bit taller and fill out a bit. They were gigantic.

It wasn't long before the shouting and cheering started and along with the noises from the wrestlers as they slammed upon the canvas and threw each other into the corner posts, you couldn't hear yourself think.

I shouted and cheered with everyone else, occasionally looking at Mum to make sure that I still had her approval and wasn't overstepping the mark. I needn't have worried, she was too busy watching the action. The first two bouts were over (too soon for my liking) and the interval came, which was my cue to take my pen and autograph book and wait outside the changing room door. I soon had three of them and it was time to take our seats for the second half. I didn't mind, as there would be time enough at the end to get more signatures. I made a mental note to look at the local paper next week. They were sure to have a write up and a few photos in there, after all, the reporter and photographer from the Stroud news and journal were not there for nothing. I would be sure to cut it out and put it on my bedroom wall.

The last bout finished and we had about 30 minutes

to wait for the bus, so with Mum's permission, I was back outside the changing room with autograph book and pen at the ready. I did well that night, eight wrestlers, the referee, the two seconds, Master Of Ceremonies, the timekeeper and (much to his amusement) the caretaker of the hall. Oh boy, my schoolmates were going to be envious in the morning. I was silent all the way back on the bus as I recalled everything, in great detail, that had happened that night.

When we arrived home, Dad was waiting up for us and had a pot of tea ready. So as I sat sipping this welcomed bevy I retold the whole episode to Dad. He just smiled and nodded as I explained that we had seen a real Red Indian fighting a real Cowboy in the ring before my very eyes. "Did you all enjoy it?" asked Dad as he glanced around the room and for the first time since arriving home I realised that nobody else could have got a word in. "Yeah great" said one of my two older brothers, "except for Mum". She stifled a laugh. "Let me guess" Dad smiled. "She made a fool of herself, didn't she?" We all laughed. My brothers sang out in unison "she was totally embarrassing!"

Mum rose to defend herself. "Well that horrible man was hitting that nice one behind the referee's back and I thought that was wrong."

Brother Pete spoke up. "That was no excuse for hitting him with your handbag. Look at it. It's all twisted."

"I know," she said. "I had a heck of a job to open it to get the bus fare out."

I well remember the hidden smiles as I announced to the family that one day I would become a wrestler.

Over the next year or so we saw many bouts of wrestling on a monthly basis at our local hall and even some of the well-known fighters of the day at the nearest larger Cheltenham Town Hall, including some of my heroes from the television. My autograph book was getting well used and full to the brim. I made a mental note to myself to include a new one on my Christmas list. Apart from Leslie Philips and Frankie Howerd, it was full of wrestlers.

At the age of fourteen I decided that what our village needed was a group of young would-be wrestlers. So off I went armed with several bits of old rope and much to my mother's annoyance (once she found out) several bed sheets from the airing cupboard, and set out to find four suitable trees with the right distance between them, so that I could make my very own wrestling ring. I had to hurry as I had all my mates arriving within an hour or so, to put on our village's first of many wrestling bouts.

It's surprising what you can do with a few sheets and a bit of rope. OK, we only had one rope, but rope is very hard to come by at that age and it did make it easier to put up and take down, especially if it started to rain. Never mind, one day I would own my own proper wrestling ring, but in the meantime, it would have to do.

Over the next couple of months we fought each other over and over again. My mate Clive would be the timekeeper, as he was the one who owned a watch, and Tony would ring the bell for the rounds to start and finish. It made sense, as he had to travel the furthest so he always had his bike with him, which sported a rather convincing bell.

It became compelling Sunday entertainment as we would try and emulate what we had seen the day before on World of Sport. Sometimes I would be Billy Two Rivers and sometimes I would be the Masked Outlaw. However the forays came to an abrupt end when Mum found out about her bed sheets. Was I in trouble over that! I was confined to my room for the whole week and there was talk about me missing the television wrestling on the Saturday, but she relented at the last minute, I think I had washed up on one occasion and managed to get back into her good books.

I was not deterred though. From that time on we would have to wrestle on the grass, but at least we still had a rope. Well, until my brother wanted it back, and then it was a case of just putting your jumpers on the floor and guessing where the sides of the ring would be. It worked for goalposts so why not wrestling posts?

That seemed to keep us going until that fateful day when it all came to an abrupt end. When the football season started, everyone vanished. I quickly realised that wrestling didn't actually mean that much to my mates and that it was impossible to wrestle with yourself without being put into a special jacket and taken away to the funny farm.

The months went by with occasional trips to the town hall to see my heroes in the flesh. Then one night my older brother Pete came home with the news that he had joined a boxing club about an hour away, and was I interested in going? I thought about it and came to the conclusion that although it wasn't wrestling, at least I would be able to set foot in a real ring, which was something I had wanted to experience for a long time now. Just to stand up there and look out at the cheering crowd was compensation enough, considering that I would probably get my head punched in. So there I was, on the back of my brother's motorbike in the middle of winter, freezing cold and about to do something that didn't interest me. In fact, I stuck at it for ages. Well it seemed like ages, but in fact it was about three months. I did what any self-respecting boxer would do. I won the first fight, lost the next four and packed it in. I guess I wasn't cut out to be a boxer.

Good old Pete, he hadn't given up on me. He informed me that he was off to Birmingham at the weekend, as he had found out that a few of the wrestlers went to a place called Hadley Playing Fields every Sunday morning to train and would I like to go with him? I was over the moon. In six days' time I might well be able to pick up a few tips from the big guys, which would be sure to give me a good start when I finally found myself on the road to fame and earning the respect from others that I had lavished upon my heroes at every opportunity. After all, six days was nothing – wasn't it? Wouldn't you know it - three days later I came off my pushbike and smashed some bones in my right arm. My world had come to an end.

I still went however, and enjoyed every minute of it, especially as I had seen Reg Yeats, Johnny Diamond and the great Pat Roach many times in the past and here I was standing next to them and hearing them talk wrestling. It didn't really matter that I had my arm in a sling. They welcomed us and spent time explaining things, how and why they train. They showed us some moves they had been working on and answered all of our questions and believe me, there were quite a few.

On the way back I sat in silence and thought to myself. As soon as my arm was better, that was it. I was going to do whatever it took to turn this pathetic young lad into a person that future fans of the grappling game would come to respect. Come hell or high water I WAS going to do it, though when or how, I had no idea.

It wasn't long before I took my first step on the ladder. Well - I thought it was. The promoter came up to me one night at our local hall and asked if I would be coming to the next one in a month's time. He must be joking. Nothing on earth would make me miss it. And so it was that I was given the very important job of… selling raffle tickets. OK, it wasn't a big step but it did mean that I would get a free ticket to the next month's show and as far as I was concerned I was in.

During the next few months we were finally able to persuade Dad to come along. "Only if I have your solemn promise that your Mum won't show me up" he said. We promised, and even suggested that Mum should leave her handbag behind. We needn't have worried; Mum was on her best behaviour. She didn't even make a fuss when Dad was up at the ringside banging on the canvas demanding that the coward in the blue corner should be disqualified. Yes, he had caught the bug, and was even worse than Mum had ever been. Even the man on the door had to tell him to calm down and stay in his seat.

It was a very long and quiet bus journey home that night. It wasn't until we had all reached the familiarity of our own living room that we all burst into fits of giggles at Dad. Who would have thought that such a quiet, mild-mannered man could get so worked up? But nevertheless he had enjoyed it and was to become a regular grappling groupie like the rest of us.

Three years passed, and I was about fifteen years old when one day a young chap called Ken came to our house to mend the television. We joked with him about the breakage and told him that it wasn't Dad attacking it on Saturday afternoon that had caused the damage, and very soon the conversation got around to the wrestling. Ken assured us that it was just a valve that had blown and quickly mended it.

Over a cup of tea we got talking about the wrestling. He said that he quite fancied having a go and that he was visiting the Gloucester travelling fairground next Saturday, as they had a boxing and wrestling booth there, and did I fancy going? Like a shot I leapt at it, and true to his word he picked me up and off we went. The boxing booth was at the far end of Gloucester Park, which is a large, open space on the outskirts of the city centre where the travelling fairground would visit once a year. The booth consisted of a large tent that attached to the one side of the lorry and the bed of the lorry was where the owner stood.

"Ladies and Gentlemen!" he shouted through a microphone. "Roll up, roll up! Tonight we give you two bouts of boxing and two bouts of wrestling. First we have the boxing. Is there anybody here tonight willing and brave enough to go three rounds with my boy here?" And so it went on. Once the billing had been filled we all paid our money and went up the steps, across the bed of the lorry and down a ramp on the other side and into the tent. Once inside we saw all four bouts before exiting back into the open air.

"What do you think?" said Ken, "Shall we have a go?"

What had we got to lose? I hadn't come this far just to walk away from it now. "Yes of course we should" I replied, and we looked around for a sign to tell us when the next bout would be.

The notice on the small blackboard informed us that the next show would be in an hour. So two hot-dogs later, a wander around the rest of the attractions, and we were back in the front row of the new and expectant crowd listening to the voice over the microphone once more. This was the last show of the night, so we looked at each other. It was now or never.

As luck had it, one of the wrestlers who had been there before had gone home so a quick word with the owner and me and my mate Ken were to fight each other.

"There is a slight problem," whispered Ken. "Whatever you do, mind my teeth."

"What do you mean?" I said.

"I've got false teeth" was the reply.

I thought this was a great start to my soaring career, made even worse by the owner coming up to us and asking if we had boxed before.

"What do you mean?" I said, "We are wrestlers."

"Oh no" came the reply "I thought you said boxing."

This was eventually sorted out and we ended up in the right ring. Now the time had come for me to break in my new wrestling boots that I had purchased only a while ago and show some of the skills I had learned from watching others. All I had to worry about was Ken's teeth.

Three rounds of three minutes in length later and

we had done it. The referee had announced the match a draw and Ken's false teeth were intact. We left the ring to tremendous applause from the fifteen or so people that had actually paid to see us. We collected our fee, which was a ten shilling note each, and left with the sound of applause ringing in our ears, OK, thinking back, the appreciation was not so much for the skill we had shown in the ring but more for the fact that we actually had got up there and had a go. However you looked at it, I think it's safe to say that as far as wrestling goes I had well and truly opened my account.

I spent the next couple of days thinking of that first bout, recalling every move and thinking to myself that had it been now, how differently I would have done things. Hindsight is a wonderful thing.

All the fun of the fair

The fairground was there for two weeks, in which time I never missed a night. By the end I was fighting not only every night but sometimes twice, and on a couple of occasions three times. More often than not my mate Ken was there, but as I explained he was married with a young family so had other commitments. I understood this and so I ended up in the ring with quite a few experienced wrestlers who had been in the game a while. Through my eagerness and commitment, they gave me all the encouragement they could. I discovered that they had been wrestling for some years but had not wanted the travelling involved so would turn up whenever the fairground was in town.

By this time we had got to know the owner well and

I soon realised that we were actually dealing with a legend in fairground circles, or a showman, as they were known. Ronnie Taylor not only worked the wrestling booth but the helter skelter and a few other sideshows as well. On our last night in Gloucester Park we found out that their next destination was the Hereford Cider Festival. This was a huge attraction to Hereford, the hosts being a well-respected cider company. There would be celebrating in the streets, as all the centre of the town was closed off to traffic and all sorts of attractions brought in which included the wrestling booth. Rumour had it that in previous years the cider festival had boasted, as their centrepiece, a fountain of cider in the town square, but previously, a chap had been so drunk that he fell in and drowned. I never did find out if this was true or not, perhaps they were just pulling my leg.

Ken and I had already made up our minds to attend and on our third day there we were invited into Ronnie's caravan. "I'm very satisfied with you, boys," he said in his Welsh accent. I wasn't surprised. Between us we must have netted him a fortune. "Do any of you fancy coming to work with me full time and travelling around with us? We've got about four weeks until the end of season and we could do with wrestlers of your standing." (I think he meant cheapness.)

Ken said no straight away, which I was half expecting - after all he had a steady job and family to consider. I, however, was what you might call between jobs, and was eager to accept. So it was decided that I would meet up with them in a week at the County Fayre in Stourpaine (somewhere in Dorset). That gave me a clear week to sort out things at home and be on my way.

That was a late summer in my youth that I would never forget. Not only did I gain a lot of ring experience, I met some of the kindest people I have ever known. I know some people form their own opinions of the travelling show people, but I would be less than truthful if I didn't say that I found them extremely honest, kind and thoughtful and very considerate. The downside to all this was that I had to tell my parents of my decision, and they were not happy about the news at all. I had just started as an apprentice cabinet-maker with a small family-owned business, something my parents were pleased about. The despair in their voices when I told them I was giving it up spoke volumes. Believe me, I was not the most popular son of all time. Fortunately, they eventually relented and accepted the idea, saying that if I was that stupid then I had made my own bed and I must lie in it. So, suitcase in hand I left home for a new adventure. Only time would tell if I had made the right choice.

My first introduction on arrival, having hitched a lift all the way, was to have Ronnie take me into his van and utter the words "feed that boy". Those words have stayed with me all my life. I later found out that he was the hardest bloke to get money out of, but he would feed you until you bust.

"Right boy, now let's see if we can find you somewhere to lay your head" he said. He took me around the lorries and generators to a small caravan situated at the back of all the bustling noise of the fair. He knocked politely on the door and a lady answered. "Oh hello Ron" she said. He cleared his throat. "Got a young boy here joining us. Can you put him up?"

I smiled at her and she gave me a toothless grin. Well I think she was a her, because I couldn't help noticing that she was sporting a full beard that Captain Birdseye would have been proud of. I was later to find out that her name was Mary and by some quirk of nature she had grown a beard and was now making her living the best way she could by becoming a fairground attraction.

That first surprise over, I was faced with another one almost immediately as two lovely young girls of 19 years of age were introduced to me, also as my living companions. "We've been working for Ron all season" said one. "I'm Marilyn and this is Becky. We're the strippers." I must have looked a sight with my mouth wide open and my skin the colour of a beetroot. To say that as a young lad I had suddenly grown up and become worldly wise rather quickly was an understatement. Who else did I know who had spent the first part of his teens living in a caravan with two strippers and a Bearded Lady? Wait until my mates back home hear about this, they'll never believe me!

I later found out that both girls would also take it in turns to be Rhona the rat girl. Their day job was to sit in a cage in a scanty bikini with rats crawling all over them (pet ones of course.) While one was working with the rats, the other would be dressed as Frankenstein and would sit in a dimly-lit tent in a mock-up of an electric chair, pretending to be a dummy. When enough of a crowd had filtered in, she would suddenly jump up and leap off the little raised stage and frighten the punters nearly to death before getting back in the chair and becoming a dummy again.

I quickly learned that a showman's life was a busy one, up at the crack of dawn every day cleaning and checking all the equipment and making any repairs needed as well as replenishing prizes, carrying coconuts, replacing light bulbs and the unenviable task of putting goldfish into little polythene bags. If it was a relocation day, there was even more work to do. Pack up everything and strip down rides and sideshows (everything had a place and an unalterable routine) then a long drive and set up (usually overnight) in the next venue and so it went on all season, finally culminating in everything being taken back to the outskirts of Gloucester where we were to sit out the winter. I stayed on at the end of the season to help with any refurbishments that were needed and managed to pick up several skills, including woodwork, painting and a not insignificant amount of signwriting. (Which I might add I have called upon at several times in my life.)

All in all, it was deemed, by yours truly, a great success and as good a way as any to reach my final goal. I lost count of how many fights I had taken part in, but this was greatly enhanced by Ronnie promoting me to booth boy. Roughly translated, this meant that I would stand up on the booth and with the help of the right banter from the boss, take on all comers. This varied from like-minded youths such as myself to alcoholically-enhanced members of the general public who had come straight from the pub and were intent on impressing their girlfriends or mates. The latter became the easier of the two, probably due to the fact that once they were face up on the canvas, those that didn't throw up all over you were too far gone to get up under their own steam. My favourite way to dispatch a drunk in the ring was to grab his arm, spin him around a couple of times, then throw him backwards against the corner post. Those that didn't pass out would usually give up. What a way to make a living!

I managed to secure the following season, with the fairground work during the day and fighting at night. My new-found family of showground people were a pleasure to be among. I can't say that I socialized much with them as there was little time, but nevertheless I made some good mates.

It was toward the end of the second season and I was in my usual position on the booth taking on anyone who fancied their chance when I heard a familiar voice from the crowd say, "I'll take him on." I glanced down and saw my old mate Ken smiling up at me. Suffice to say that the bout took place and afterwards we had a good old catch up.

"How long have you got to run now?" he said. I reported that I had another ten days to the end of season, then it was back home. "Give me a bell when you get back. There's someone I want you to meet" he said. Eventually he took his leave and I went back to my evening duties.

About two weeks later I found myself sitting in his front room with a cup of tea in my hand and my fairground life firmly behind me. "I'd like you to meet Roy Harley" said Ken. "He lives in Gloucester and he's thinking of starting his own wrestling promotions business. He wondered if you would be interested in joining."

Roy was a well-dressed, dapper man in his mid-thirties who seemed to know what he was talking about. He knew the wrestling game inside out, except that he had no desire whatsoever to step inside the ring himself. He stated that promoting would be something he could do in his spare time, as he already had a busy job attached to Heathrow Airport on security which occasionally took him abroad, so he could not make unlimited commitment, but was I interested in what was on offer?

A thorough discussion into the wee small hours began, to end when Ken finally called it a day, saying that he had work in the morning and the televisions of Gloucester would not repair themselves. The three of us met several times over the next few weeks and eventually thrashed out a system that would suit us all. We managed to team up with several like-minded people from Gloucester, Yate and Bristol, and so Associated Promotions was born. There was however a slight problem. Roy had succeeded in purchasing a ring, but it was a boxing ring and would need to be modified. To do the alterations, there was a small snag. We would need somewhere big enough, and the only place was Ken's garden. Little did we know what we were letting ourselves in for.

A wrestling ring is 16 feet square (I've often wondered why they call it a ring) and this boxing ring was 24 feet square. The centre support of a wrestling ring was built of several upside down "A" frames, while a boxing ring was made of box sections - four ropes for boxing and three ropes for wrestling. It doesn't sound much when you say it quickly, but it meant nearly three months of hacksawing, welding (neither of us had welded before), drilling, painting and generally grafting, every weekend from dawn till dusk, until we had it done. I will never forget that time. I think I still have callouses on my hands to prove it, more than forty years later.

For three months, I had worked on the building sites in order to make ends meet and I now found myself doing every task from putting in drainage pipes to laying roof tiles and slates. It may have been a long three months, but the different skills I picked up are still with me today and over the years they have contributed to saving me thousands of pounds by enabling me to do jobs for myself. Even now, one of my main hobbies is DIY, and I owe it all to that struggle to build that damn wrestling ring.

It was at this time that I decided that what I needed was a new image, so I took a long hard look at myself. It is not enough to get into the ring and fight, you have to be entertaining, so I looked at some of my heroes. The most popular were the ones who were so skilful that they left you full of admiration at their dexterity. There was no way I could begin to put myself in the same class as them. I faced the fact that I was never going to dazzle the audience with skill, so I decided to dazzle them with a look. I thought of some of the fighters that had done the same. I remembered Ricky Star and Adrian Street, two wrestlers I had often watched. They would enter the ring, bright in colour, sequined tights and complete with make-up. OK, so it was a somewhat camp image, but it had worked for them, so why not me? After all, I had the long hair. All I had to do was to dye it blonde - and what could be easier, as my girlfriend at the time was a hairdresser.

I shall never forget the look on her face when I announced that I wanted to become blonde. Once she stopped laughing and realised that I was serious, she gave it some thought. She did take some persuading though, and made sure that I knew what I was getting myself into. If my hair fell out due to the peroxide, it was not of her doing. It would shock the audience, I thought. I was right; it even shocked me when I first saw the result. Oh well. It was for a good cause, and anyway there was no going back now.

I also managed to persuade her to make me a new gown for entering the ring. I remember it well. It was in a bright red corduroy fabric which reached the ground and buttoned up to the neck, with a black imitation fur collar and matching sleeves. I had purchased some silver boots with silver Lurex tights and matching trunks, and with her help, the latest in Max Factor make-up. I was either going to get lots of work or be locked up. I wasn't sure which.

Next I needed a new name, as I had already worked out that most wrestlers used a 'stage' name. I mean it doesn't take long to realise that Chief Thunderbird wasn't born to Mr and Mrs Thunderbird and christened Chief by his parents. I needed a name that reflected my ring persona. The name of Johnny came to mind (later to be changed to Jackie) and as for a surname, I selected Evans. I still don't know to this day why I chose it as a surname, but as it was used on posters, I guess I became stuck with it. Never mind, it would be as good as any and I can say now, forty years later, that I have never had cause to regret it. So that was it. Jackie 'Glitterboy' Evans was open for business.

Next I would need some publicity photos, so off I went to the nearest photographic shop to make the necessary appointment. "What did sir have in mind?" asked the shop assistant. "Oh just some pose pictures for the posters" I replied, trying to keep the actual details as vague as possible. The photographer would know on the day, but I didn't relish telling the receptionist and have her laughing in the shop.

The appointment was made for me to attend a shoot (as it was called) on the following Saturday at ten o clock. I was in plenty of time and stood in the shop with my small case, waiting my turn, when out came the photographer. He was a man of small stature wearing a tweed jacket, pink shirt with matching cravat. He walked over to me with what can only be described as clenched buttocks and shook my hand limply. (For those of you who haven't guessed what was coming next and those of a delicate nature, please look away now or at least turn over a couple of pages.)

To say that I was nervous was an understatement, but he showed me into a little changing room next to the studio and left me to it. A million thoughts must have gone through my head at that moment. "What the hell am I doing here?" I muttered to myself as I pulled on my silver lurex tights. "I must be bloody mad", I thought as I reached for my make-up.

I finally plucked up the courage to enter the studio. He looked me up and down with one hand slightly higher on his hip than seemed healthy, and with a high pitch to his voice, said "Hey ho, let's go then." There followed the most embarrassing twenty minutes of my life as I was encouraged to stand with legs apart, hands on hips, give a little pout, blow a kiss or two and stick my bum out for the camera.

Finally, In what seemed to be a lifetime, it was over and it was a wrap (as they say). I did break all records in getting changed into my normal clothes and made a quick exit, stopping only to hear when the proofs would be ready to view. This could be done at the front desk, which was welcome news, I can tell you.

Within a few days the proofs were ready to be viewed and once selected, I had the prints a couple of days later. My mate Ken roared with laughter as I relayed my experience to him over a cuppa. "It's not over yet, matey," he said. "You know what you've got to do now, don't you? You need to get some of the mannerisms right if you're going to be convincing, and there's only one way to do that. You need to spend a bit of time studying in a place where they all meet up. I believe there's a bar in Gloucester."

I stopped him in his tracks. He was right of course, but it would have to be a bar that was a bloody long way from where I was known. A few discreet enquiries came up with the name of a bar about thirty miles away where I could do my homework in the knowledge that I would not be known by anyone. It was a fair way to go for a pint of shandy, but no way was I going to take the risk. If any of my mates found out, my life wouldn't be worth living.

I formulated my plan of action on the journey. I would sneak into the pub and order a soft drink in my deepest voice possible, then find a table in the corner where I could observe from behind my copy of *Rugby News*. After all, who would ever suspect my reason for being in such a bar? I felt comfortable in the knowledge that only I and my mate Ken knew about it.

My mate Ken, yes my good mate Ken. He had stitched me up like a kipper. As soon as I arrived and opened the door, there was a big cheer as several people shouted, "It's Jackie Evans!" or, "Come on in Jackie, we've been expecting you." And so it went on. Ken had telephoned the barman earlier that night and explained what was to happen and why.

I must admit, despite all that had happened, they were a great crowd and much to my surprise I felt very comfortable with them all. That is until I went to the bar to get another drink and bumped straight into, yes, you've guessed it, the flipping photographer, who apparently lived five minutes away. So much for my undercover work. But they were very interested in what I was doing with my wrestling persona and to be honest, I think a few of them felt quite flattered that, as one put it, I was fighting their corner. I left with the solemn promise that I would look in again, and as for my mate Ken, boy, was I going to get him back.

Before I pursue my narrative further I feel that I have to set the record straight with regard to the world of professional wrestling. As you might imagine, over my twelve years as a professional and indeed right up to present, the question that most people ask me is "is it fixed?" I have to say here and now that the answer to that question is a definite NO. (I cannot however vouch for the modern sport, as I simply do not know enough about it.) But certainly in my day none of the bouts I knew about were fixed, rigged or pre-arranged.

We do however have to look logically at this. I myself have met and fought many of the names of that era and can say that apart from one (more of that later) all of them were nice people, and as with any job be it in a factory, office or anywhere else for that matter, I made a lot of good, true friends in the same line of work. They are your workmates and each one of them needed to work in order to live. Many of them had families and dependents. And I, along with most of them, was not in the business of inflicting terrible injuries on someone for the sake of it.

That apart, when we had our opponent in a hold we all did our best to damn well keep him there for as long as possible and try and beat him the best we could. I did know one wrestler, a household name at the time who shall be nameless, who would try and dispatch his opponent by some quite lethal methods, with the result that in the end, no one would fight him. It wasn't through fear though, it was just that he had become a liability to all those making a living at this game and wrestlers would not risk being out of the ring for a time and losing their living. Consequently the bloke in question got less and less work and finally disappeared from the ring altogether, never to be heard of again.

Of course there was always the odd time when two people had a bit of history between them and this would show itself in the ring, but these were not common throughout the game and they were soon sorted with a few words from the promoter of "sort yourselves out or get out". I hope I have managed to put to rest those myths that the wrestling game had been blighted by for so many years.

As I have said before. Jackie 'Glitterboy' Evans was now open for business. It wasn't long before Associated Promotions were hosting their many events in smaller town halls, leisure centres, local fetes and special functions. Even the odd village hall was used if it was able to accommodate a ring and enough seating to make it worthwhile.

In the six years that we were together we must have staged the best part of 550 wrestling shows all over the South West of England, and I'd like to share with you some of the best ones that still stay in my memory today. Some were good, some were exceptionally bad and some were total disasters. For whatever reason, they have stayed with me and so I am happy to share them with you.

Knocked out by a little old lady

Very early on in my time with Associated Promotions, I realised that if my strategy of playing the 'gay boy' was going to work I would have to be the villain. Accordingly I adopted the usual punching behind the referee's back, kicking my opponent when he was down and various other ways of gaining an advantage and clearly upsetting the audience to the point where they loved to hate me. It doesn't make you a popular bloke in the bar afterwards, as you'll hear later, but it's good for business. After all I've got a living to make and a job to do.

It was about three months from starting when we found ourselves fighting in a town hall somewhere in Somerset. As I remember, I was up against one of the local wrestlers. All was going well and the crowd was getting annoyed with me. I had been gaining the advantage by whatever means I could. I got him in a head lock, turned my back to the ref and proceeded to land a few choice punches to his face, making sure the crowd on that side of the ring could see what I was doing. I did this a further three times so that the whole audience could see what I was up to, resulting in an uproar of disapproval and complaints to the ref. Once or twice people in the front row came up and banged on the canvas, in a fit of protest to the referee. I looked down my nose at them, tossed my head in a carefree way and shouted at them to "Sit down and be quiet." I then grabbed my opponent, held his face on the top rope and proceeded to rub his eyes across it. At this point, they were going wild, calling for me to be disqualified. This sort of behaviour continued for a further two rounds when all of a sudden, my opponent managed to grab my arm and throw me against the corner. Then with a body slam I was face up on the canvas near to the ropes and then, well I don't remember what happened next but the next thing I knew I was coming round back in the changing room with a damp towel around my head.

Little birds seemed to be flying around inside my head and tweeting profusely, while in contrast, a dull ache accompanied it on the other side. I felt as if a raging bull had trampled me.

I sat up and saw a lady standing over me. "What happened?" I enquired. The promoter came over, "You were out for the count." (By this time I had made it to my feet.)

"You're joking! My opponent was the other side of the ring. How can that have happened?"

The boss man laughed. "You were mugged." By now he had lost me completely. I scratched my head, luckily, a part that didn't hurt very much.

"What are you on about, mugged?"

"Someone at the ringside belted you over the head with an empty pint mug."

"Where is he now?" I asked, gritting my teeth.

"Don't worry it wasn't a he, it was a dear old lady. She's with the ambulance people, they are calming her down. At least she did the decent thing and let her husband finish his beer before she grabbed the glass. The ambulance men want to take you to hospital and the police will want to talk to you. Are you up to it?"

"Yes I'm fine. Bit of a headache though. Can you tell the police that I don't want to press charges?"

"Are you sure?"

I knew full well that the last thing I needed to read in the papers was the headline 'Wrestler Knocked Out By Grandmother'. That would not do my career any good at all, and can you imagine the ribbing I'd get from all the others?

"There is one good thing," said the boss,"You didn't break the mug. Could have been quite dangerous with people rolling about in glass, you might have ripped the canvas!" He was laughing.

The story did however have a satisfactory ending, because the local papers ended up showing a picture of me with my arm around the lady with a headline saying, 'Mrs Mercer still enjoys wrestling at the age of 82' and a bit about her background completing the article. I still don't know to this day how the promoter managed to convince the two guys from the local paper that this lady's age and background were a better scoop than her managing to drop a wrestler with a pint mug, but I am glad he did. It cheered me up no end to think that a promoter had earned his money for a change.

I did however draw the line at presenting the lady with a bottle of sherry. "If you think I'm going anywhere near her when she's got a bottle in her hand, you can think again" I told him.

As for the head, that got better in a day or so despite the riot act read to me by the ambulance man who was not happy with the fact that I had refused to go to hospital. I tried to explain that I had to get home as I had another bout the following night. Years later I would come to understand the seriousness of a head injury, but as a 17-year-old boy I just passed it off as one of those things. It wasn't the first time it had happened and it wouldn't be the last.

Incidentally I was knocked out five times during my wrestling career and none was by an opponent. It was always by an irate lady at the ringside. In addition to the pint mug I was despatched with a glass ashtray, a rolled-up umbrella and two handbags, all in separate parts of the country. I must have been quite convincing as a baddie. It just goes to show that, even in the name of entertainment, you can still push things too far.

Eventually, I would learn to control the situation caused by my underhanded ring tactics and get to know, by instinct, how far was too far. I was a very quick learner – or at least I was once I had received a few more hard knocks to the head.

Not so gay as she thought

We were wrestling in a little village called Ruardean Woodside, somewhere outside Cinderford in the Forest Of Dean. My memory of this one is quite plain, helped by the fact that I now have a poster on my wall of this very show. It is showing its age, but then aren't we all?

The first bout was The Tomahawks, 'Masked villains of the ring', versus The Silent Ones from the Midlands. Second up was Joey Marciano from Cardiff vs Pete Preston from Luton. Then came Billy Drummond from Durham vs Terry Fear from Bristol, and then yours truly vs Tony Whaite. I remember this one well. There were some lovely people in the Forest Of Dean who took their sport seriously and always enjoyed their wrestling. The night went well and at the end of the evening most of the wrestlers retired to the local pub for a well-earned pint. Being in a small community, we chatted into the wee small hours to several of the locals. Some who had been in the audience that night were a friendly bunch and conversations went from wrestling to local places of interest, from football to the annual village cricket match. Were we, as wrestlers, interested in putting up a team to take on the locals on their charity day, then eventually back to wrestling?

At about 11.30 pm word came that one of the chaps who was taking down the ring had severely cut his hand and had been taken to casualty in nearby Gloucester. Great, I thought. There goes my lift home. I remember that at that time I was having car trouble and had secured a lift with one of the crew. It wasn't long before a young chap who had seen us in the ring offered to take me home as he lived near to where I was staying. He reported that it would be a bit of a squeeze to get me into his modest but comfy car as he had promised a lift to a few others, but he would get me in somehow.

We all carried on socializing for a while longer and finally the landlord called time. True to his word the young lad was ready to sort out our travel arrangements and after a bit of trial and error three lads were in the back seat, so would I mind if I sat in the front and put his girlfriend on my lap? That was fine by me. She was a pretty little thing with long legs that went right up to her seatbelt.

"Is that OK with you?" I said to the driver.

"Yes that's fine, I mean if I can't trust you, who can I trust?" He was referring to the fact that, by what he had seen in the ring that night, I was gay. "No offence intended" he added.

I felt at that point that I should have said something to make it clear that actually, I was not gay. But I did not want to put my lift home in jeopardy, so I kept quiet. I did as I was told and sat in the front seat, and this chap gently lowered the mini-skirted girlfriend into position on my lap. This young lady, who was, to say the least, tipsy, couldn't get comfortable, and to my amazement (and I have to say to my growing enjoyment, if you get my drift), she kept wriggling around...

About halfway through this interesting journey the driver enquired if anyone minded if he smoked, and did anyone happen to have a light. "I have a lighter in my pocket" said I, "but I can't get to it." I suggested that the girlfriend should be able to reach it for me if I moved ever so slightly to the right.

I had a very interesting five minutes with this young tipsy girl rummaging in my trouser pocket trying to find my lighter. Finally, I had to say that I must have left it at the pub. What was not mentioned was that, although he thought I was gay, I had left his girlfriend in no doubt that I wasn't.

Finally, I got out of the car at my destination. As I waved them away I remember thinking that perhaps I should have done the decent thing and told him that I didn't smoke and had never owned a lighter in my life. I always smile when I recall that particular episode and thank the lord that I never had a lighter, because I'm sure that it would have exploded in my pocket.

I can't remember the name of that good Samaritan and I never even got to ask the name of his girlfriend which, in the grand scheme of things would have made me, shall we say, less than a gentleman.

The show must go on

I don't remember the date but it must have been in the summer months, as I recall it being a very hot day. I had picked up a bug that prevented me from eating much without feeling sick. What was worse was that any food that did get into the digestive system seemed hell bent on completing the cycle in top speed.

As I was not yet able to afford to live on the wages I was getting from my fights, I did what most people did and took a day job. The only ones that suited my lifestyle were in the building trade, so I often found myself on a roof during the day and in the ring at night.

One day I was sent home by the gaffer, who told me in his broad Irish accent, "I don't want any more workers off sick and I don't think the Portaloo can take much more of you." He was right of course, but that didn't help with the fight I had that night. It was too late for me to rearrange the billing – besides, the posters had been out for a few weeks and tickets sold on the strength of it, so it wasn't fair, let alone a good business move, to let anyone down. There was nothing for it. I would just have to go through with the fight.

I took myself off to bed for the remaining hours that were available to me before it was time to get ready and leave for the venue. I didn't manage to sleep much as most of the time I spent tripping backwards and forwards to the loo.

Eventually the time arrived for me to get ready. I took a shower, dressed and checked my tools (what we called our wrestling kit.) Then I checked the diary to see where I was fighting and who with. Imagine my dismay when I saw that I had to travel to somewhere in Bristol and was fighting a bloke named Russ Healy. Now I had known Russ for many years and we had fought together many times. In fact, he was the chap who had loaned us his welding kit a while before when we were converting the wrestling ring. He was a really nice chap, but when he was in the ring he took no prisoners. When you fought Russ, you knew you had been in the ring with him. Nothing serious or dangerous, but the next day you would appear to have more than your fair share of rope and canvas burns. It was possible to beat him, but you would have to work hard at it. On that day I couldn't work hard - my insides had already reminded me of that during the day at regular intervals. We were already at the toilet roll in the fridge stage.

I set off earlier than usual, as I felt that this time there would have to be several stops before reaching the venue. However, as I remember, the journey seemed quite uneventful in spite of the situation and I arrived in plenty of time. As I sat in the changing rooms sipping at a glass of water, Russ came in with another fighter and was complaining about someone who had upset him during the day. He was clearly not in a good mood, as he passed me with only a quick nod of greeting. Oh God, I thought, I'm going to disgrace myself in front of a couple of hundred people tonight and end up doing something very childish in my trunks.

As time ticked by other wrestlers arrived and I explained to a couple of them my situation and, yes, you've guessed it, I got no sympathy at all. In fact they spent all their time taking the mickey, which was no more than I should have expected. Someone suggested a commode in the corner, another a brown canvas. One even offered to go to the local chemist and get me some nappies. I didn't rise to it. I just sat there like a wet blanket and drank my water. After all, there was always a lot of ribbing between wrestlers and it was always someone's turn. Tonight, it was mine.

It was time for the first bout and I was on second, just before the interval. Oh well I thought, at least they will have the interval to clean up. It seemed no time at all before I was due in the ring. It appeared to be quite a way to the ringside but I can honestly say that for the first time since I had started to wrestle as a gay boy my mincing walk to the ringside that night was for real.

I rather gingerly stepped into the ring, paying particular attention to how I lifted my leg over the ropes, when all of a sudden there was a bump and a cry of pain from the other corner. There were people milling about and fussing, so I went to take a look and it seemed that for the first time that day, Lady Luck had shone on me.

Poor old Russ was in a heap on the floor, holding his foot. Eventually the medic was called and the Master of Ceremonies announced that this bout would not take place due to Russ 'The Rebel' Healy tripping up the step and sustaining a possible fracture of the foot.

I returned to the dressing room a happier man than perhaps I should have. But thanks to the misfortune of my fellow man I could still hold my head up in wrestling circles.

I saw Russ on several occasions after that and told him of my situation on that fateful night in Bristol. "Oh I knew all about that from the other blokes and I was looking forward to giving you an extra big bear hug somewhere in the second round" he said with a wink in his eye.

It wasn't long before Russ was back in the ring, even though he had broken two bones in his foot. I had completely recovered in just two days, which just goes to show you can't keep a bad man down.

Take my family - please

Later on in my career, I would spend time wrestling at holiday camps. It was a natural progression in the grand scheme of things. However I hadn't been wrestling very long when I had the opportunity to ply my wares as a one-off at a well-known holiday camp.

After fighting, we would stay overnight at the camp

and travel home the following day. I was able to get a lift to the venue from a couple of wrestlers I knew from my fairground days. I drove to Bristol and left my car at their house and we all piled into the same vehicle for the two-hour journey. To say that it was a squeeze was an understatement, as there was Trevor and his brother Mike (who formed a tag team), Trevor's wife and his mother and yours truly, all crammed into this little car. Trevor was an amiable sort of chap and his brother (who had been deaf and dumb from birth) seemed OK, a bit of a ladies' man by all accounts. Trevor's wife appeared to be the kind of woman who took no nonsense from anyone, and his mother, it seemed, could have picked a fight at a nunnery. Such were my companions of the day.

"Now look, ladies," said Trevor, "in all seriousness, this is the first time you've come to the wrestling with us, and I want you to promise that you won't show us up."

"I don't know what you mean, our Trevor" said his belligerent mother.

"You know exactly what I mean" he replied. No more was said, which immediately got me concerned. What had I let myself in for?

The journey was uneventful, apart from the odd outbreak of bickering among the family from hell, which, thank goodness, did not involve me. We arrived at the camp and checked in, that was me and Trevor, while the two women headed straight for the nearest bar and the brother headed off in the other direction looking for crumpet (and I don't mean the food kind). Trevor, who by now looked a worried man, turned to me and said "Look, Jackie, I'd like to apologize for my family."

"What for?" I asked.

"Well, nothing yet but I just thought that I would get it done here and now because, knowing that lot, there's bound to be something before long."

We found our chalet and got settled in. We had about three hours to kill before the afternoon show, so I decided I would get some food and perhaps take a swim. So with towel and trunks in hand, I headed off. I came across a small little café just opposite the outdoor pool and so I decided to eat there.

As I sat with my burger and chips, I couldn't help noticing a bit of a stir outside the bar opposite. I sat there and watched as two burly men evicted his wife and mother from the premises. Poor old Trevor, I thought, so that's what he meant about apologizing in advance.

Food eaten and newspaper read, I started off for my swim. Ten minutes or so later, Trevor came by. "I suppose you've heard, have you?"

"I've heard nothing, Trev. I did see them from the café window though. What did they get kicked out for?"

" Oh no, I didn't know that! When did that happen?"

"About ten minutes ago, what are you on about then?" I asked.

"My dear little brother Mike. Trying, in his own sweet way, to get into a lady's knickers. He got caught by her husband."

I was shocked. "No. Where was this?"

"Never mind where, it was who, that was the problem. It was only the wife of one of the other wrestlers in the tag team we're fighting later. What a bloody mess!"

I tried my hardest to stifle a laugh but managed to keep a straight face as I asked him if there was anything I could do to help.

"Nah, thanks for the offer but I'm just off to see him now, I'm going to have to sort things out" he said.

I leaned on the edge of the pool and watched him go, looking like he had the weight of the world on his shoulders. Some family day out for him, I thought as I resumed my swim.

The atmosphere in the changing room could have been cut with a knife. In fact, I was glad to get into the ring and away from it for a while. Fighting an eighteen-stone opponent was like a walk in the park compared to the tension of the changing room at that time.

When my bout had finished and the main bout had started, I decided I would quickly shower and change and perhaps go for a well-deserved pint in the bar next door. I should have stayed in the hall because, as I was to learn later, all hell broke loose during the main tag match, which, given the events of the day, was to be expected. I could not have been more wrong. Apparently, the wrestler with the wayward wife had been thrown clear out the ring by Trevor, and immediately set upon by a few people in the crowd. There were punches thrown and chairs thrown and general mayhem ensued, culminating in him finishing up on the floor minus his trunks. It just wasn't his day, was it? I couldn't help feeling that poor old Trevor's relatives had something to do with it, but then, we would never know.

I made myself scarce for the rest of the day and night and left them to it. I did however arrange to meet Trevor for a nightcap later. I managed to amuse myself with a show and then a film and finally a pint in the bar with Trevor, where he relayed some of the antics that his family had got up to and who they had upset since last we spoke. All of this I managed with a straight face. We finally had to make our way back to the chalet, where the others were totally exhausted from their rampages of the day.

As we entered the chalet, all seemed quiet. "Finished for the day, have we?" said Trevor to the women. " No riot police? No water cannons?"

His mother spoke first. "Haven't you noticed, our Trevor?"

"Noticed what?"

"Outside the door."

He said nothing and we turned and went out. We

both gave a start as we saw, hanging from the telegraph pole, the trunks of the wrestler Trevor had fought. Both the women had been instrumental in de-bagging him on the floor during the hullaballoo earlier that day. "Bloody hell!" said Trevor as we returned to the chalet. Turning with a venomous look to his brother, he said, "I suppose you've got his wife's knickers as well, have you?"

That was just too much for me and I collapsed into a chair in fits of laughter. "I'm sorry Trev, I've just spent the whole day trying to keep a straight face about this, but I find the whole thing bloody hilarious" I said.

"Don't you encourage them" he said in a voice of resignation.

"Come on, lighten up. Nobody's been hurt in any way, it will all be forgotten in a day or so. Don't take it all to heart, mate" I replied.

Mother chimed in, "See, even the little poof finds it funny."

"Yes," I pitched in, "even the little poof finds it funny."

"Don't you laugh too much" said his wife. "It's not too late to de-bag you and have your pants flying on the pole."

I beat a hasty retreat to my room and locked the door, and we all settled down to a good night's sleep. That was my one and only time at that particular venue and it was a few years before I met up with Trevor and his brother again. I was thinking of asking him how his family were keeping, but I thought better of it.

Things that go bump in the night

This particular evening I remember well as it was to repeat itself later in my life (about forty years later, in fact.) We were staging an evening of wrestling in a town somewhere between Cardiff and Swansea, I can't remember which. The evening started as many did, quite uneventful from my point of view. The second bout of the night was under way, then it would be the interval, and I was first bout in the second half. I was standing at the back of the hall watching, as we often did, when I heard loud voices in the entrance foyer. I went to investigate, along with the promoter, and found the caretaker talking to three men at the front door. There didn't seem to be any trouble, but they were deep in conversation. It wasn't long before the promoter was at our side and joining in.

It seemed they were in the old house next door trying to do a paranormal investigation, and all they could hear was the wrestling going on. It appeared they had waited months for the opportunity to gain permission to investigate this particular dwelling, and there was no other night they could do it. The caretaker, trying to defuse the situation, made his apologies and assured them that it would be over at about ten thirty.

With the permission of the promoter he invited them in to see the remainder of the show at no charge.

"On one condition" said the leader in a cool Welsh accent. "We will call off our investigation until eleven o'clock provided a couple of your wrestlers come next door with us and take part in our investigation."

"No problem" said the boss. "You'll do it won't you, Jackie, and take that new bloke Clive with you?"

I relayed the conversation to Clive during the interval. "Do we get a choice?" he asked. "Not if you want to work again" I replied.

So that is how we found ourselves in a dark and somewhat unfriendly haunted house in the early hours of one Saturday morning somewhere in Wales. Luckily I found it very interesting, and I'm sure Clive did once we got him to stop shaking. We spent what seemed like hours sitting in a dark room while the leader called out "Is anybody there?" I seem to remember that we did hear several noises through the night, but as to whether they were of this earth I honestly couldn't say.

"Neither can we" one investigator said, "not until we get a chance to examine all the data we've collected." He went on to tell me about all the equipment that they had placed around the building, which apparently would kick into action the minute anything set it off. I'm sorry to say that most of his explanation went over my head, but I did the decent thing and just smiled and nodded at the right moments.

One thing that did become apparent was that it would have been impossible to perform these tasks with a wrestling match going on next door. It must have put their sensitive equipment into overdrive, to say the least.

At about 3.30 am I started to nod off. I was sitting in a nice comfortable chair in the dark, which at that time of the morning seemed to be the sensible thing to do. I suddenly came to my senses. For no reason that I could see, the door to the room had suddenly slammed.

"What the bloody hell was that?" said Clive. I could tell from his voice that it had shaken him as much as it had me.

"The door slammed" I said. The funny thing was that all the others were in the room with us. As I was nearest the door, I thought some of them might have thought I had had something to do with it. I would have in their position, but I was the only one who knew that I hadn't.

I needn't have worried. They simply said it wasn't unusual to have this happening, and they were expecting a damn sight more before the night was over. I took a big gulp and said in a higher voice than I had meant to, "Oh good, I can hardly wait".

I must say that to my mind, nothing else happened for the remainder of the night, although as I said, they would not know the extent of their success until they had examined the data. We said our goodbyes and Clive and I left and made straight for the nearest all-night diner. After a huge breakfast and a couple of mugs of tea, and a rather lively discussion about what we had witnessed, he went his way and I went mine. I had a long drive ahead of me to my next venue and more important, my digs and bed. I thought to myself that one day I would like to look into what I had experienced and see if I could find out more.

Forty years on I now go on regular paranormal investigations with my dear friends in Gloucestershire, run by the 'Gloucester Ghost Lady', Lyn Cinderey, who is one of the kindest, generous and most thoughtful people I have ever met. If ever you find yourself in Gloucester I would encourage you to treat yourself to a ghost walk around that great city. You will find it fascinating, as well as getting to meet the great lady herself.

The mystery smell

The Hillbilly was a wrestler who I only came across once in my whole career, but believe me he was never to be forgotten.

It was around about Christmas time and we were doing a show in Shaftesbury in Dorset. Shaftesbury is a pretty little town and is best remembered for Gold Hill. We older people recognize it as the location used for the Hovis advert on the television when a young lad dressed in short trousers and a sleeveless jumper with a flat cap pushes his old delivery bike up a steep, cobbled hill to deliver bread. The hall we were in was at the top of this hill, and I remember standing in the ring and being able to see right down this street. It was a beautiful setting.

I don't remember who else was on the bill that night but whoever they were, they would have remembered that particular show.

I was on first bout, so I was back in the changing rooms in plenty of time to meet the one called the 'Hillbilly'. He was a pleasant enough chap and stood in his ring attire of dungarees and straw hat. There was however a terrible smell coming from him that no one could place, which made for a very uncomfortable time in such a small room. When the interval finally arrived, every available door and window was opened. Without referring to it and chancing upsetting him, it was plain to see that he too, was uncomfortable with the situation, and we began to wonder if it was he who was the source of this awful odour, or perhaps it was coming from some other source.

Most of us spent the interval trying to locate the source of the smell, to no avail, but we noticed that when the first bout after half time was underway, it seemed to have moved from the changing room to the main hall. Even the people in the first few rows were starting to shift in their seats and fan themselves with their hands and anything else that came to hand.

Nobody could get to the bottom of this awful smell,

but after this bout everything became clear. As the last two wrestlers were getting ready to take their shower, there was a shout from the shower cubicle of "What the hell?" We all rushed forward to see what had happened and suddenly, all became clear.

The Hillbilly, who worked in a garage in his home town, had realised that if he were to leave work at his usual time he would be really pushing it to make it to the hall on time. So he had decided to change into his ring costume before leaving. By his own admission he had been taken short on the journey down and was forced to relieve his bowels in a wood on the side of the road. Once finished he pulled up his dungarees without noticing that he had deposited the majority of his load in the back of this garment. He had continued his journey wondering what the smell was and thinking it was probably due to the rural setting he was driving through.

The thought that he had then continued to wrestle in this condition and not be aware of this unfortunate situation filled him with remorse and I had to admit to being one of those onlookers that were filled with the humour of it and laughed about it for weeks.

After that episode, if one of us needed the toilet just before going on (as more often than not we would, thanks to nerves), we would just say, "I'm off for a Hillbilly." For many years after, I enquired among the other wrestlers whether anyone had heard of the Hillbilly, but no one could recall him (apart from those of us who had been on the bill that night). I never heard of him again and have even searched all the wrestling records I could lay my hands on, but to no avail.

Working with promoters

It was about this time in my career that I felt a boost was needed. I decided that the time had come to step up a notch. I was getting a reasonable amount of work from Associated Promotions, but if I wanted to become a full-time fighter I would need to take on more work.

My past experience had told me that I needed to contact as many other promoters I could think of and creep, toady, grovel and generally fawn over them to gently persuade them that I was the man for the job. This, however, proved more difficult than it first appeared. Anyone who thinks all promoters are built of the same stuff could not be more mistaken; never before have I dealt with such a diverse bunch of people. They varied from perfect gentlemen to the downright rude, with everything in between. OK, I guess they are in the business of making a living, and it soon became evident that they were all sprinkled with the "what's in it for me" dust, but one or two of them expected their wrestlers to travel hundreds of miles to fight and be grateful for the money that was on offer even though it wouldn't have paid for your dinner. Thankfully those promoters were in a minority and did not play a part in my career. They were quickly forgotten, not only by myself but by every other wrestler that I knew. In fact they very soon went out of business.

That aside, I met several of the better ones and would like to share them with you, as these were the ones responsible for eventually spreading the world of wrestling into all the local town halls and city halls and indirectly for bringing the game to the box in the corner of your living room.

Before I talk about the good guys, there was one so-called promoter I contacted who did seem to give me a rough time. As I recall, the conversation with - let us call him Mr X to save his family any form of embarrassment - went something like this.

"Hello, is that Mr X?"

"Yes. Who is this?"

"My name is Jackie Evans. I have been wrestling for a few years now and I just wondered if you are taking on any more fighters on your books?"

"Just a minute… (long pause)… oh yes, you're that poof from Gloucester aren't you?

"Well yes that is my gimmick."

"We don't want your sort in the game, mate. Wrestling is about big burly blokes, not people like you. It's blokes like you that give this game a bad name."

"Well actually sir, it's blokes like me that put bums on seats"

"No it ain't , it's your sort that *****s people off. I don't need you in my mob, so ****off." (Puts phone down.)

Cut and move forward seven years; the phone rings.

"Hello, is that Jackie?"

"Yes it is."

"You probably haven't heard of me, but I am a wrestling promoter and I'm very keen to put some work your way if you are interested?"

"Can I ask who's calling, please?"

"Yes, it's Mr X."

"Really? Well Mr X, I have heard of you and I happen to know that you are in danger of losing your holiday camp franchise unless you sign up some known names, is that right?"

"Well yes that's true but I am offering a good package. You won't get a better deal anywhere else."

"You don't remember me do you, Mr X?"

"I'm not sure."

"Then I'll jog your memory. About seven years ago I called you up and asked for work and you told me that you don't work with poofs. Does that ring any bells?

" Mmmm. Well, seven years is a long time but I had a feeling it might be you I spoke to. I guess it's too late for an apology?"

"I guess it is."

"But I promise you that the package is good. You would be a fool to pass it up."

"Oh really. So I'm not just a poof, but a fool as well? I might as well tell you here and now that I have just signed a contract for the promoter who is taking over your franchise, and if I'm a fool, how come I know that you've already blown your chance to provide the fighters for next season and you're out on a limb with no way back? Mind you, it's just as well. It's blokes like you that give this game a bad name." Then I put the phone down.

OK, so it might have been childish on my part but it felt damn good. I later heard through the grapevine that Mr X is no longer in the wrestling game.

However, as I said earlier there were more, good than bad and here's a few of the characters I have worked for earlier in my career.

Orig Williams

Orig was a nice chap who, as the name suggests, came from Cardiff in Wales. He was always ready to take on new wrestlers who would provide good entertainment and all-round value for money. I first met him back in the early days when as a boy I would sell the raffle tickets at our local town hall for the price of a free ticket for the next time they were in town. Not only did my trial bout go well, I found myself fighting with and alongside some of my heroes from my past, Bronco Jack Cassidy, Jim Moser and Chief Thunderbird, to name a few.

Yes everything was rosy except for one thing. I should have realised this at the time but hey, I was young and foolish.

"You're a good lad" said Orig one night as we shared a pint or two in a bar. "Where in Gloucestershire do you live?" he said. He knew of course that where the posters said you came from was not always where you lived. I told him - big mistake. "Oh you're not far from the Forest of Dean then?" he said. I admitted that I wasn't. "Great. Come with me a minute."

We went out to his car and he opened the boot and proceeded to pull out a great big roll of posters. "In that case you won't mind running these around Chepstow for me, will you. It won't take you long. There's no rush as long as it's before next Saturday".

I was well and truly caught. "Er yes, OK. What about the petrol?" I enquired.

He pulled out a can. "Here you go, there's a gallon in there, you should need about half, so let me have the other half back with the can next week in Tewkesbury."

I truly hope his ears were burning as I trudged through a snow-covered Chepstow on that Saturday morning with an arm full of posters and a freezing cold can of paste and brush visiting every billboard, lamp post and shop window in the vicinity. To add insult to injury I wasn't even on that particular bill.

Orig never got his half gallon of petrol back, but I did return the can, as he wouldn't let me forget it until I did.

All in all, Orig was one of the good guys and a pleasure to work with as well as being a very good wrestler. I'm sure he would have made it to the top had he not been involved with the promotional side of the business.

Evan R Treharne

Of all the promoters I met over the years, Evan was unique. So enthusiastic was he for the wrestling game that making money was the last thing on his agenda. He also ran a wrestling and boxing magazine called *Ringsport* which sold thousands of copies each month. It kept fans and fighters in touch with what was happening in the game and was appreciated by all. Such was his enthusiasm that I have known him put his hand in his own pocket so that others might enjoy the evening, spent at one or other of his events. No one came away disappointed at one of Evan's shows.

Evan, as I remember was one of the first promoters to introduce women wrestlers to the ring, a very good move on his part. As you can imagine it went down well with the audiences and it wasn't long before other promoters followed suit. I have to say that the females I saw fighting were very entertaining and indeed good at their sport. I always felt it was a shame that they were never taken seriously in those days and should have been given more television time. But of course that was years ago, before the term equal opportunities had been introduced.

Evan was also instrumental in bringing some of the top names into the smaller venues. And to get such names as Jackie "Mr TV" Pallo appearing in a village hall somewhere in deepest Wales was quite something. I worked for Evan many times and will always remember him fondly, and with the great respect that he deserved.

Duke Badger

If ever there was a man who could be called "The typical promoter", it was that legend of a man Duke Badger. Known throughout the wrestling fraternity as "The Duke", his forward planning and meticulous approach to detail were exemplary. He traded as Bull Ring Enterprises and obviously resided in Birmingham, but before I turn him into some sort of a demigod, he did have one fault. From the first time I met him, I remember him coming into the changing rooms at the end of the evening and uttering those dreaded words feared by all wrestlers: "Sorry lads, a bad house tonight, you'll have to take a cut in wages." There would be uproar from everyone, wrestlers, seconds, as well as the referee. This would go on for about ten minutes and eventually he would give in and pay out the wages in a downtrodden manner. Of course we soon learned that this was a try on and anyone with any sense could have quickly worked out that he was in fact coining it. I have known venues so full that there were people standing three deep at the back to watch the show, but you could guarantee that at the end of the night, there he would be with his "Sorry lads…"

I was always grateful to him though, as he introduced me to a couple of the nicest people I would ever meet, the Klondyke Brothers, Bill and Jake. They were not real brothers, although they looked it. They were both of huge stature, in fact Jake weighed in at 24 stone and Bill at a whopping 32 stone. Over the few years I knew them, Bill was often missing from the ring because of a back problem brought about by his sheer weight and size and towards the end, he rarely ventured out of his home town of Malton in Yorkshire. There was talk going around that despite his size he was a first-class flower arranger and would spend his spare time preparing some amazing flower creations for local weddings etc. Having got to know the man I can quite believe it, as many will tell you that he had a softer side to him that a lot of people never knew.

I was lucky enough to spend many hours with Jake (more of that later). As for the "Duke", he must have been either very brave or very stupid to tell wrestlers of their size and ability that they had to take a cut in wages, but I guess we all got used to his ways. It was a small price to pay for being involved with the man who, after all, was a legend.

Peter Gillott

It would be wrong of me not to include among the promoters my own older brother Peter, who, as you may recall earlier in this book, played a part in my wrestling beginnings, taking me to training at the Hadley playing fields in Birmingham and so forth. It was however a long time before I would wrestle at one of his shows. I had been fighting for quite a while then, but I suppose I was and always will be the younger brother and was somewhat overlooked as a serious contender in his eyes.

I was however allowed to act as a second, which meant that I would get the job of sponging down wrestlers at the end of each round. (Well, somebody had to do it.) I also took on the job of timekeeper occasionally, getting to ring the bell. Hardly a taxing task for someone who had, by then, probably spent more time in the ring than he had. I have to say though that he was a good wrestler and could hold his own against any opponent who was around then.

Eventually, probably because he had been let down at the last minute, I was promoted to referee, and there I stayed pretty well until the end of his promotional career, with the exception of the last few months, when as a result of wrestlers not turning up for various reasons he was practically forced into using me in the ring. The time I spent with Pete accounts for many of the memorable experiences I share with you in this book.

Peter 'Lord' Macey

During my time in the ring, especially in the earlier days, most of the promoters had some degree of character about them, but none more than Peter Macey, or the Lord, as he liked to be called. He was tall and (not my words) as barmy as they come. He would strut around looking every inch the typical squire, wearing a suit of tweed, a paisley bow tie and socks pulled high over his trouser legs, with a monocle in his right eye. He would talk with a plum in his mouth (which I knew was put on for the benefit of others, as he would invariably drop his aitches and put them back into the conversation as needed).

The other thing about 'Lord' Macey that set him apart from the rest was his ability to stage wrestling shows in the most unlikely settings. One I remember was at a wedding. We were to be the star attraction (after the bride of course). The venue was a cricket field, so it was in the open, except for the cricket pavilion and a great big marquee, and we all stood at great risk of getting soaking wet.

Before this though, he had promised the bride and groom, who were big wrestling fans, that we wrestlers would give them a guard of honour outside the church. There we stood at the allotted time, freezing cold and in our wrestling gear with our towels raised to form an archway. I felt a right plonker, I can tell you. The wedding photographer made a great deal of it and of course it made the local paper, much to the amusement of the whole village. I'll tell you what happened next later in this book. There were many "off the wall" bookings with this particular promoter and you never knew what was coming next.

These are just a few promoters I encountered over the years and I was fortunate enough, to work for them all from time to time, giving me as much work in the ring as I needed in order to take it seriously, and indeed to be taken seriously. Unfortunately, some of them have faded from my memory over the years (I can still just about see their faces but I can't remember their names). Others I probably have chosen to drive from my recollections due to some altercation at some time. Well, even the most placid of us can't get on with everyone, can we?

I would now like to continue sharing with you some other memories from my days in the ring.

Playing for laughs

I forget the venue, but I'm sure it was north of Watford. It was deep in the middle of winter, and we were due to perform in one of our usual places. I remember it well because it was one of those winters when we seemed to have more than our share of snow.

As luck had it, my brother and I had been on the bill the night before at a venue only twenty miles away and we made it to the hall without too much effort. When we arrived, our old friend and fellow wrestler Klondyke Jake greeted us.

"How goes it, mate?" I enquired.

"Well there's some good news and some bad news. The good news is that they came and put up the ring last night. The bad news is that we are the only ones here and it doesn't look as though any other wrestlers are going to be able to make it through the snow."

By this time the hall was filling up. As they were all local people they had braved the elements and made it through the snow, but it didn't seem likely that any more wrestlers, or the referee, were going to get there.

"Right then" said brother Pete, "let's look at our options. We've got a hall full of people, three of us here, and we've got to put on a full evening's entertainment. It can't be done, let's go home."

"OK" said Jake, "so are you going to go out there and tell them that you are happy to give them their money back? Because I wouldn't."

"Mmm, good point, here's what we do then..."

As it turned out it was the most memorable evening that I can recall and I have recounted this tale to many of my friends over the years. It went something like this.

"Ladies and gentlemen, welcome to our show of wrestling this evening. My name is Jackie Evans and I am your compere for this evening. Due to the adverse weather conditions, I am also your referee and your timekeeper. And if that's not enough, I shall be selling raffle tickets in the interval. Can we have the first wrestlers in the ring please."

Jake and Pete entered to tremendous applause, Jake as himself and Pete in his usual kit plus a mask made out of an old pair of black tights (I never did find out where he had got them from). I had to think on my feet.

"In the blue corner from Birmingham, please welcome Klondyke Jake. And in the red corner, from Gloucester, it's…" (slight pause by yours truly) "The Yeti!"

The crowd roared with laughter, as by then they could see that we were struggling. Then came the second bout.

"Ladies and Gentlemen please welcome in the blue corner, from Gloucester, Pete Gillott. And in the red corner from Birmingham…" (another pause, as I saw that Jake was wearing the mask this time) "The Snowman!"

By this time the audience were falling about laughing. All went well and that was another one in the bag. Bout number three was easy as far as I recall, it was Jake versus Pete without the mask. By this time everyone in the audience, and us, were fully aware that the mask was fooling no one, and the crowd appreciated it even more. The dafter the evening got, the more they seemed to enjoy it. There are several people who think all wrestling is acting - let me tell you, I was acting my socks off that night.

Then came the final bout of the evening. What the heck would we pull out of the bag for this one? As far as I could tell we had exhausted all the combinations available to us. Then Jake came into the ring to take up his position in the red corner and Pete arrived and in the blue corner, he placed a chair and left. Oh good lord.

"Ladies and Gentlemen" I uttered in a somewhat squeaky voice. "For your main bout this evening I give you, in the red corner and not a complete stranger to you I'm sure, please welcome Klondyke Jake. (I took a deep gulp of air) and in the blue corner, one half of that famous tag team, the Chippendales!" (standing ovation.) "Please welcome Chip. Or is it Dale? No, it's Chip."

That had to be the longest bout of my life as I watched for fair play between Jake and a chair. Even through the light-headedness of the situation I managed to give the chair a public warning. This turned out to be funnier than you would imagine, and at the end of the night our job was done. We even got a standing ovation from that grateful crowd. They thanked us profusely as they all vied with each other to buy us drinks at the pub over the road. They had appreciated the fact that we had not let them down even though we had few resources.

I wrestled in that hall quite a few times after that evening and always entered the ring to a very special round of applause and a few knowing winks from a grateful audience. Once, I even brought a fold-up chair and placed it by the ringside, to thunderous applause. It took some explaining to the other wrestlers, who were oblivious to what had happened on that snow-ridden night some months before.

The battle for Brean Down

I remember this particular venue well, not so much as memorable night at the wrestling but more as a nostalgic trip. We were to wrestle in nearby Weston-Super-Mare, which in itself is a lovely place to spend the day. For me, it was a great place, as I used to spend my childhood holidays in Brean, which is just a few miles away. As I drove to Weston on that day, I recalled some of the wonderful times I had spent there. One that stands out was the day when the local attraction for any young lad, the go-kart track, was closed for the day. What was I going to do without my daily fix of thrills and spills? We would race around the track at what felt like 100 miles per hour, overtaking and outsmarting each other in return for what appeared to me a very fair price of two shillings for a whole five minutes. I must have handed over a fortune over several years of visiting, and could probably have bought a go-kart of my own for the money I had spent. However, there would be no racing today as apparently they were going to use the track to take photographs of some pop group. Ah, those early days when everything was simple and straightforward. It didn't seem to matter that the pop group in question was none other than the Beatles. I was not allowed on the go-karts, and that was a tragedy.

There was nothing to be done but hang around the caravan all day and sulk. I think that it was Mother who suggested that we all go for a long walk and see what was at the end of Brean Down. The Down is a great lump of rock that sticks out into the water, dividing Weston from Brean. I remember it was a long way to the end, and as you got older, the journey seemed longer.

Now I had left home in plenty of time to reach Weston at around lunchtime and planned to spend a few hours in the area which had become a major part of my childhood. I arrived in good time, and after a quick look over the campsite we had frequented years before, I drove on to the beginning of the Down. Having first, stopped at the café for some lunch, I started the long climb up the grass track to the main track that would take me across the top, to the end. I knew from experience that this was not a short stroll, and it would probably take a good 30 minutes, even if I got a shift on.

I hoped it would not have changed, as one memory I had was of the old World War Two army camp there. I had spent hours running in and out of the derelict buildings that inhabited the rock end.

It was still there, though in a worse state of repair, of course. I stayed a while and satisfied myself with a good look around. Soon it was time for me to make a move. This wasn't a holiday after all, and I had a job to do and a living to make.

I started back with a cheery heart, stopping only to take a breather and to look at the marvellous view. Eventually I reached the end, and before making my way down the track to my awaiting car, I took one last look around.

A big mistake. My foot slipped and down I went, rolling over a few times before I came to an abrupt stop against a clump of gorse. A few onlookers asked if I was OK. "Yes fine thanks" I said, as I stood up. Of course, the embarrassment would have made me say I was OK, even if I wasn't.

I eventually reached my car, and as I put the key in the lock, I felt a searing pain from my wrist. Oh god, I've broken it, I thought to myself. How the hell was I going to fight tonight? I strapped it up with an old towel, torn into pieces (not an easy task with one hand out of action) and in a considerable amount of pain, drove the several miles to the venue. There was no time to visit the local casualty. By now I was in a good deal of pain.

"What have you done?" said one of my fellow wrestlers when he saw my wrist wrapped up in bits of old towel. I relayed my news to him as I unwrapped it, finding that it had swollen considerably from the time I had bandaged it. He checked it over.

"Shake my hand," he said.

"You must be joking" I replied.

"Trust me. Just try it. You've got nothing to lose, have you?"

I made to shake hands and he grabbed it with both hands. I heard a click. I nearly wet myself and was just about to give him a mouthful of abuse when I suddenly noticed that it wasn't giving me pain any more.

"You just pulled the joint out of alignment" he said. "All sorted now, it will be sore for a while but at least you can use it."

He was right of course. Apart from the soreness, I was still able to use it and indeed fight with it. Apart from the odd twinge in the ring, it felt OK.

That was my first taste of having another wrestler 'repairing' me before and after a bout. I have performed similar treatment on other wrestlers over the years. It was always just a part of the job. Luckily, my opponent that night didn't get to hear of it, otherwise he might have played on my wrist to his advantage.

It was at least 35 years before I found myself at the foot of Brean Down again. My wife's cousin and his family live down that way, and it was a weekend away at a family christening that enabled me to visit. This time, I would not be climbing my way to the end of the rock - nothing to do with my injury of course, that was healed and forgotten years ago. It was the fact that I was now aboard the fast train to retirement that finally decided it.

We did manage to check on the go-karts however, they were long gone, as with many other things from my childhood memories. The campsite was still there, now trading under a new name with some lovely up-to-date caravans.

No room at the inn

Promoters are a clever breed of people, and never more so than when it came to making money, or more to the point, saving it. It was no more evident than when we were on what was to be known as a "package." This is when, through a bit of wheeling and dealing, a promoter would put on four shows over four nights, in four venues, within a 20-mile radius. They would put eight wrestlers together who would fight all four venues, but would change opponents every night. The promoter would do a deal with the owner of a guesthouse and book all concerned into the same place, at a reduced rate of course, saving on travelling expenses.

On this particular package, the venues in question were around Grantham in Lincolnshire. All the venues were easily accessible, and the guesthouse was more than acceptable.

The first show went without a hitch and we were counting our blessings that we, at least, had time on our hands to look around the area and spend our days at leisure. After a particularly pleasant day spent in the countryside, the five in our party of sightseers decided it was time to head back and get ready for the eight-mile journey to our second venue.

As we pulled up in the car park we noticed something unusual. The three of our group who had decided to stay behind were waiting for us with all of our bags outside the door to the guesthouse.

"Where the hell have you been?" asked Billy, one of the lads.

"Why, what's happening?" we asked.

"We've been kicked out" came the reply.

"Why?" we all sang out together.

"Dunno, something and nothing really" said Billy. " Although it might have had something to do with the owner coming home and finding me in bed with his missus."

I have never seen Billy run so fast around the car park with five irate wrestlers chasing him, threatening what we were going to do to him when we caught him.

We tried to secure new digs in the vicinity but it soon became quite clear that mine host had been on the telephone to his fellows within that area and no one would take us. A variety of reasons were given, but we were not daft, we knew we had been blacklisted. We finally found another lodging house some miles away, though lord knows what the promoter was going to say when he finally got wind of what had occurred. The best thing was to sort it out the best way we could.

We did our other three nights without a hitch, as Billy managed to keep a low profile. I don't know what the promoter said to him at the end of the run, but we were all reimbursed for the money we had spent on new digs and the extra travelling. It was thought that the extra money came out of Billy's wages, although the promoter would never confirm this. Billy was never heard of again on the circuit, of indeed any other wrestling venue that I was aware of. Perhaps he had decided to call it a day. After all, he must have worked at least half a week for no money.

If by any chance you are reading this book, Billy, take a bit of advice. Don't do it again - or at least, don't get caught.

A shocking encounter

As I may have said before, not all our escapades were purely innocent. After all, we were young lads in those times, and boys will be boys. The next adventure is one of those I shall always remember, as long as I live. We had just finished an evening of wrestling somewhere in the Yorkshire Dales (the actual place escapes me). I had met a young lady who, probably because I was a wrestler, had taken a fancy to me, and me being the randy young devil that we all were in those days, I decided that it would be a good idea to take her out for a drink after the show. It turns out that she was 23 years old, which was a year or two older than me, but who was counting.

We had a couple of drinks, (cokes in my case because I was driving) and on the way home, we decided to have a kiss and cuddle in an open field. It was a balmy night in the middle of summer, so it seemed a good idea. We stopped the car and climbed over a gate at the side of the road and within a few minutes were busy entertaining ourselves on this shallow bank. I'm not going to explain any more as I'm sure that you get my meaning.

Many years before that, when I was at school and had reached that age when we were taken to one side and instructed in the ways of the birds and the bees, we were told not to, and told that we shouldn't, and what could happen if we did, and told that it was probably best to wait a bit before we tried, and so on. I remembered all of this information, but one piece of advice I don't recall - there was no mention of what to do when you put your bare ass onto an electric fence.

I cannot begin to explain what it was like. Suffice it to say that we had obviously been sliding down the bank at a faster rate than we thought. It did however, put the lid on any further dalliance that night and we both dressed rather rapidly and made our way, somewhat shakily, back to the car, where we both burst out laughing. I know an electric fence won't kill you, but it does tend to limit your romantic intentions.

I did the decent thing and dropped her home, never to meet her again. I went on my way to my next venue with the feeling that for at least ten minutes, I could have run two electric hair dryers and possibly a twin tub.

A long wait for breakfast

It had been a good night in Yarmouth and the venue was

filled, with standing room only. A good variety of wrestlers had provided the entertainment for the night. Autographs had been signed and the crowd had dispersed in a happy mood. A quick drink and chat with the lads and then back to the guesthouse a couple of miles away. I arrived back in time to cadge a cup of cocoa from the lady of the house, then dived into bed for a good night's sleep. Life was good. Tomorrow would see me in Cardiff, then a couple of days off.

Morning came around as quickly as it does and I was up, packed and ready to go to breakfast. I entered the dining room to be greeted by a few smiles and the odd good morning to the other guests and took my seat at a table and waited. And waited… and waited….

Mumblings from other guests informed me that they had also been waiting. I went to the kitchen to see if anyone was about, while one of the other guests decided to go and see if our host had overslept. There was no one in the kitchen, so I took my seat again. The other guest came back and informed us that he had knocked on the door and after receiving no reply had tried the door. Inside he had found the lady in bed. Unfortunately she had died some time during the night.

All we could do was ring the police, who then had relayed the information to the key holder, who happened to be her son. He was quickly on the scene and busied himself with the policeman, covering such formalities that were needed in such a situation. All we could do was to sit and wait as we were informed that we might be required to make statements, depending on the cause of death.

Nearly two hours later, with a lot of hungry people milling around, the doctor arrived and after ten more minutes informed us that she had died of natural causes. With the agreement of her son, who was naturally distraught, a couple of the ladies who were guests managed to rustle up breakfast for us all while I and another guest sorted out our payments for the stay.

Within a couple more hours I was on my way, along with others who were leaving that day. We had given our condolences to the son before we departed and wished him well.

I have often wondered whether the place continued as a guesthouse. I hope so - as those establishments go, it was one of the better ones.

Rings and things

This story comes to mind not because of its humorous or quirky content but because it may serve as a reminder of how easily things can go wrong, and also, how seriously wrestling fans take their sport.

Some wrestling fans were more than happy to shake you by the hand and ask for the occasional autograph, some were happy to buy you a drink. There were, however, those that wanted to organize a lynch mob and would like nothing better than to see you hanging by your neck from the town hall clock.

During the holiday season, it was not unusual to find that a good amount of work came from the seaside areas as opposed to town halls. We had been frequenting the lovely little seaside town of Lyme Regis for a few years as I remember and had some good audiences there. The promoter had been approached by a committee member of the nearby town hall of Seaton with a view to taking our shows there for the remainder of the season, and if all went well, for the years to come.

A date was set by mutual agreement with all parties and within a short time, we had been booked for this particular venue. I discovered that I would be lucky enough to be in Lyme Regis on the Tuesday and Seaton the following day. I reveled in the fact that I could stay overnight and enjoy a day by the seaside before making that short eight-mile journey to my next fight.

All went well in Lyme Regis. I enjoyed a leisurely breakfast at the hotel before taking a stroll around and enjoying the hospitality and the views on offer. I sat and chatted to a number of people, strangers to me but people who had been in the audience the previous night, so felt that they knew me enough to talk to. I took afternoon cream tea with a middle-aged couple from Daventry who had met some of my colleagues in their home town and proceeded to tell me that if ever I found myself in their neck of the woods then I should be sure to look them up and stay the night with them - after all, they would be going to see the wrestling anyway.

Eventually I said my farewells and proceeded to Seaton, hoping to be there in plenty of time to see a few sights before arriving at the town hall for work. I left Lyme Regis for what I thought was a short journey, but about a mile outside the town my luck ran out. After two diversions due to roadworks, getting lost several times due to a total dearth of road signs and on top of that, car trouble, I arrived in Seaton twenty minutes late. I eventually found somewhere to park, about ten minute away from the town hall. I knew that I was second bout on the bill and that would give me about thirty minutes to get ready in total.

I knew there was a problem as soon as I entered the hall, as you could have cut the air with a knife. I dumped my kit in the changing rooms and went to find out what the problem was. There in the middle of the mayhem was Bryan. It was his job to deliver the ring to the venue and erect it in time for the show and afterwards pack it all away ready for the next venue. He was standing in the middle of the stage addressing a belligerent mass of people who were shouting and arguing with him. I arrived beside him just in time to hear him say to one chap in the front "Now look here mate, you'd better be quiet because that's fighting talk."

He turned to me and told me that he had arrived earlier on and having unloaded the ring from the van he had discovered that there were no nuts and bolts.

"Where's the ring now?" I asked.

As if by magic the angry mob parted and I could see the ring neatly laid out on the floor, awaiting erection. "Look here" I appealed to the crowd. "You must be able to see the predicament that we are in. If anyone has any ideas, we are happy to act on them to the best of our ability."

"We want our money back" they chorused. "It's a ***** shambles".

I continued, "Ladies and Gentlemen I fully agree and so you will, but please be aware that we are not the ones who took your money. That is the booking agent and he would have passed it on to the promoter. It's really nothing to do with us."

Five or six of them piped up "Where is he then?" I turned to Bryan with a questioning glance.

"He's not here, typical of him, I rang him and told him what had happened and he's told me to deal with it and that he'd square up with me tomorrow."

"Oh my god. What are we going to do?" I said.

Bryan pointed to a man in the front. "well it's not my problem, but if it helps I'm quite happy to smack him in the gob."

"That's not going to help is it?" I said as I struggled to stop the man from getting at Bryan. This was turning into a nightmare. I searched my mind for a solution.

"Look" I shouted at the heaving mass of anger in front of me. "I can only see one way out of this ladies and gentlemen. If you would care to write your name and address on your ticket and let me have them, I will see to it personally that you will get a full refund from the promoter within the next few days. Now I don't really see that I can do anything else, can I?"

As luck would have it, a couple of policemen had arrived and took to the stage, and within a couple of minutes I had informed them of the situation. "Well sir" one of them said, "It does seem the best solution." He then informed everyone that a name and address on the back of their tickets would get them a full refund and that if it didn't, then they could ring the police in Seaton as they would be in possession of the name and address of the promoter, and would pass it on to them. This seemed to do the trick and eventually the angry mob dispersed, albeit rather noisily, into the streets of Seaton. When they had all left I thanked the two officers and assured them that I knew the address of the promoter and would see to it personally that it was dealt with.

I gave Bryan a hand back onto the lorry with the ring and off he went. I did the usual security rounds of the building, then sat and waited for the caretaker. He arrived about an hour later and listened as I narrated the evening's events to him.

"Hmm" he said. "They are a funny lot here in Seaton." I must say that I was inclined to agree with him. I did hear later that the promoter had indeed repaid all the money that was owed (I personally think out of sheer embarrassment more so than loyalty). His last words to me were "I don't think I'll bother with Seaton again." It's a shame, because I'm sure it's a lovely place and given different circumstances it could have been an enjoyable place to visit. Not because of any of this, but I have never, ever been back to Seaton.

Well-travelled whisky

As I have said before, promoters are a diverse bunch. Some are generous, some not so, and one or two are downright mean. But none of them came anywhere near the miserly ways of my next subject. To save any repercussions to his obviously long-suffering family, I shall refer to him as Mr Tight.

Mr Tight was well known in the business and many a wrestler would tell you that no opponent was as hard to deal with as this promoter at payout time. Compared to getting wages from him, the art of wrestling an eighteen-stone opponent was a breeze. This came to a head one night in the Midlands and no, I have not given his name away, as this particular tightwad came from north of the border and the Midlands was as far south as he would venture. However, we had all arrived at the venue only to be told that there had been a mix-up somewhere along the way and the day and date on the posters did not correspond with the booking of the hall. In fact the hall had been booked for an old-time dance with a 1940s theme.

The caretaker, who was obviously a wrestling fan, stayed at the main door until all the wrestlers had arrived and then kindly ushered us all into a room off the side of the main hall. He supplied us with tea and coffee-making facilities as well as a few plates of sandwiches from the dance buffet. OK, the sandwiches contained spam with little or no butter, but after all, it was a wartime theme, and we were grateful for them.

As we all sat chatting together and bemoaning the fact that given the promoter's reputation, none of us were actually likely to get paid for our wasted trip, Bernie the ref, who was not only a good referee but the right-hand man to Mr Tight, suddenly leapt to his feet. "I've got a great idea, I'll be back in a minute" he said, and with that he disappeared out into the car park, returning a minute later carrying the biggest bottle of whisky I had ever seen. "Here you go chaps, get stuck in" he said.

"Where in the heck did that come from, Bernie?" we asked.

"Oh, that was to be tonight's raffle prize" he replied."

"He's gonna kill ya" said one. "That's a bit generous of him" said another. I piped up, "You'd have to sell a lot of raffle tickets to get your money back on that one."

"Oh, he has" laughed Bernie. "I've been working for him for at least four years and it's the same bottle of whisky that was here when I first came. He raffles the same one every night and wouldn't you know it, a member of his family usually wins it. I've won it at least twenty times, I would have won it tonight as well if things had gone to plan."

It was a good job the dance band was playing loud in the main hall or they would have wondered what the cheering and laughter was all about.

"Hang on chaps," said one of the blokes, "We don't want to get old Bernie the sack, do we?"

"Don't worry about that guys, I'm off to live in Canada from next week" said Bernie. "I told the old bugger last week, but he didn't believe me. I'm off to stay with my sister in London tomorrow night and fly out from there so he can say what the hell he likes, it ain't gonna bother me none. Cheers everyone, it's been good working with you. Now drink up, there's some paper cups on the tea tray. Help yourselves".

Of course none of us got paid for that night and Mr Tight never did find out what had happened to his one and only raffle prize, although he did convince himself that through dubious means it had probably ended up the other side of the Atlantic.

The night ended well though. When the organizers of the dance realised that we were there, they invited us in to spend the rest of the evening with them as their guests and boy, did they look after us. Trying to jive to the big band sounds of In The Mood and Little Brown Jug would have been quite embarrassing had we not been plied with the finest scotch beforehand.

We all reflected afterwards on the success of the evening as we tucked into a late-night oriental meal at a restaurant around the corner. A few swift black coffees brought us back to the level of decorum needed to get us past the ever-critical gaze of the landlady at our digs.

In at the deep end

Usually a memory of my wrestling days comes to mind because of some unusual or amusing event that took place. However, there were two in particular that I remember purely because of the surroundings we were expected to fight in. One was in Fishguard. I will relay that one to you in a later tale, but the first one I would like to share with you was a northern venue. Again I will not give the real name as it is not in my nature to belittle a place I have only visited a few times and to chance upsetting the local people who only ever showed me kindness. Having said that, there are probably many of my friends who have heard this one and know exactly where it is.

This venue was a great big Victorian building which housed the local swimming pool and was known as ******** Baths. Over the summer months it would be frequented by all the keen swimmers in the area and probably by the majority of schoolchildren, who either didn't mind or were forced to swim in a pool that had no heating whatsoever, and that included the changing cubicles around the edge. When the winter months arrived, the pool would be emptied of water and scaffolding erected in the pool up to ground level, whereupon sheets of boarding would be laid and fixed in place in order to turn the venue into a dance hall. A good idea really, as it made a great place for local bands to strut their stuff.

Not so good for our purpose though. The changing rooms were underneath the boards and there were two exits from this sunken hell, up the steps at either end. With freezing temperatures, manoeuvring around the scaffolding poles aside wasn't too bad if you were placed in the deep end, but look out if you picked the shallow end. Trying to get into your wrestling gear in a room that sported one dim light bulb and had a maximum headroom of three foot six inches (just over a metre) was a fight in itself. Blimey, if health and safety had reared its head in those days I'm afraid that would have been the end of that venue.

It didn't stop there - there was no seating. Even the poor old timekeeper, who had been before, had to bring his own chair and fold-up table. The problem started on the way into the ring, that is provided that you had safely negotiated the ladder and not cut your head open through the small square hole cut into the boarding or scraped all the skin off your back on the hatch cover which had to be replaced in order to stop anyone falling down there. No, the main problem was getting past the crowd of people. As there was no seating, it made crowd control impossible, and that meant no aisle leading to the ring.

The only way through was to politely mutter, "Excuse me" or "can I please get by?" As the ring was half the length of an average swimming pool away, this meant about fifty requests to get by. We all started off with good intentions, but as the journey wore on politeness turned into abruptness and finally into rudeness, which meant that by the time you had arrived in the ring you had upset quite a few of the audience. Couple that with the fact that I was known as a dirty wrestler and by the end of the bout I had severely upset and generally hacked off most of the crowd, and somehow I still had to run the gauntlet back to the safety of the hell hole which was known laughably as the changing room.

Needless to say, the crowd did enjoy the evening, and apart from dodging the odd headbutt and punch from one or two enthusiastic fans on my way from the ring to the descending ladder into the shallow end, the evening seemed to go well. However I was never asked to fight there again, which I took as a stroke of luck. I was told some years later that that building had been pulled down in order to put in a multi-storey car park and that they had since built a brand new leisure complex a couple of miles away with a heated pool.

The worst-organized evening ever

As a rule, most wrestling evenings, up and down the country, tend to go without a hitch. Apart from the odd unforeseen injury or the occasional power cut, most are enjoyed by everyone concerned. This particular event was different. After a nightmare journey to the West

Midlands, I booked into my digs as usual and having arrived rather late, I went straight to the venue, which was a short walk away.

I knew that all was not well when I arrived to be confronted by not one or two wrestlers but twelve. Even on a bad day, my knowledge of the game told me that, even with a bout of tag wrestling on the bill, we would only need ten fighters. Nope, not even twelve - another five had arrived. What were seventeen wrestlers doing in the same venue? I didn't know, and it seemed that neither did anyone else. What was more, there wasn't a wrestling ring, and a quick trip around the town revealed that no posters had been put up.

What were we to do? There was only one answer. We did what any self-respecting wrestler would do and retired to the nearest public house.

My inclination was to write the whole episode off and put it down to "one of those things", but some of my workmates were not taking this lying down and were going to get to the bottom of it, mainly for the sake of their wages. After many phone calls from the payphone on the corner of the street, we seemed to be none the wiser. There were a lot of miserable faces in the bar, with the possible exception of the landlord, who must have thought a coachload had arrived to sample his less-than-palatable ale. It was not the liveliest of pubs and the classical music playing over the sound system did nothing to lift the mood. Some of the very few locals there were perturbed at their routine and peace being shattered.

When I ventured to the bar to replenish my drink, the landlord enquired if now was a good time to take photographs and collect autographs from all the wrestlers. I quickly informed him that although I didn't mind, perhaps it was not a good time for him at the moment, as for some of us, there was a crisis happening and it was probably in his best interests not to chance upsetting some of the wrestlers further. He asked what the problem was and I filled him in with the details.

"Oh that makes sense. Just a minute." He disappeared out the back and returned in a short while with a couple of fliers. Apparently they had been delivered to him a couple of weeks before, but he didn't see the point of putting them up in the pub, as the venue was about twenty miles away.

OK, so we now knew that there had been a mix up with the venue, but what was happening twenty miles away? There must be a hall, complete with crowd and ring but with no wrestlers. Another trip to the phone box was needed. After a few minutes, the blokes returned to report that much the same thing was happening twenty miles away, except that the hall in question had two rings and about six audience members, who were demanding a refund. Why were there so few in the crowd? Simple - we had the posters at our end.

A few of us made the decision to travel to the other venue. Some of us wanted to find out what happened and one or two were on the trail of their wages.

On arrival, we were confronted with a very irate caretaker, who seemed more confused than we were. He was ranting and raving at any wrestler who came within six feet of him, which was a brave move on his part. A couple of us managed to take him to one side and inform him that although we realised the important role that a caretaker had, it was not in his best interests to take it out on these particular people unless he wanted his sweeping brush to be put away in a dark place, and we didn't mean the broom cupboard. He soon saw the error of his ways and quickly disappeared to put the kettle on.

Throughout all of this fiasco there was no sign of the promoter, who, we were to learn at a later date, was on holiday in Spain. So nothing could be done. After a cup of tea by courtesy of the caretaker, we set off for the twenty-mile return trip to explain the situation to the others. That done, a few of us decided to make an evening of it and went for a pleasant meal at a nearby restaurant, while the grumpy ones went home, more upset and angry that they needed to be. After all, these things happen.

It was a pleasant meal and finally I returned to my digs, having put it all down to experience. It was not all bad though. Within a couple of weeks, I received a letter of apology from the promoter explaining the mix up and enclosing my full payment of wages and a few pounds extra for my troubles. I assume the other wrestlers received the same. To my mind, the promoter had redeemed himself and had been more than fair in his actions and I, for one would be more than happy to work for him again.

Remember you're a bouncer

This particular episode happened fairly early on in my career but, I have only today remembered it so I am going to include it here.

One day, I and a few of my fight buddies received notification from a promoter enquiring if we would be willing to take a trip down to Bristol to a new venue which had been recently opened and do a one-off job as doormen (bouncers as they were more usually called.) This was something different. Apparently the contract of hire for this hall had a paragraph in it that stated that if they were expecting a large crowd, then it was obligatory to provide at least eight professional doormen. Nowadays there are specially-trained people who are licensed to do this sort of work, but back in the late sixties, we were the closest profession that would fit the bill. We were informed that it would be the latest and most popular group of the day that would be appearing. The money plus expenses sounded good, so we signed on the dotted line. We had to be there at four o' clock on this particular Saturday - a bit early we thought, but they were paying and perhaps there was a photo call to cover, or something like that.

We duly arrived, crowded into one large Dormobile, and easily found the car park at the rear of the premises. We were a bit early, so we decided that we should all go for a late lunch at the Wimpey Bar a few minutes' walk from the hall. We were making our way back to the venue, wondering which famous pop group we were working for, when we turned the corner to be confronted by a poster. Imagine our surprise to learn that our services had been requested by... the Wombles.

We must have looked a sight, eight grown men laughing like young kids who had been up to mischief.

Needless to say we never had to eject one troublemaker all day, but instead spent most of the time helping young mothers up and down the steps with pushchairs. It was all a bit of fun and we got into the spirit of things with funny hats we had bought from Woolworths over the road. And gave out sweets to the kids. I don't know whether it was a bad thing, but none of us actually got to meet the Wombles. Thinking about that day still brings a smile to my face even now.

The stripper

Now and then a job comes up that's a little bit out of

the norm. Much like the last narrative. This was to be a one off, certainly in my career, but nevertheless worth a mention.

To set the scene I need to tell you that somewhere in that lovely city of Bath there was, at that time, a group of what must have been wealthy businessmen who had come together to form some sort of a club. From what I can remember it was a men-only affair, which was deemed acceptable in those days. However, on this occasion, they had put together an evening of entertainment which would take place in a very opulent hotel somewhere near the heart of the city (the actual name of the hotel escapes me). There were to be two bouts of boxing, arranged by the local amateur club, followed by two bouts of wrestling. Then there was a rather grand meal with fine wines and spirits, followed by the main entertainment of exotic dancing (a stripper to me and you).

The evening started well and I remember that the four young boxers did their club proud and were a joy to watch. Then it was our turn. It seemed to go down well with all concerned; the only thing that didn't appeal to me was that you couldn't see across the room for cigar smoke (another indication of the times in which we were living). While the bow-tied gentlemen enjoyed their meal, we all gave a hand to dismantle the ring as the young lady dancer would be using the stage and anyway, we had to put seating out at the front of the stage for us (another perk of the job). After the meal was over and cleared away and the young boxers had been disgruntled at having to go home without catching even a glimpse of the dancer, the music came up. Like my colleagues, I had taken my seat and relaxed back in the chair to watch the show.

When the girl finally came on stage, she was carrying a box, which she placed on the stage in front of me. She then proceeded to extract the biggest python I had ever seen. Now I must admit, I was petrified. She then came down from the stage and placed this great big snake around my neck. It was at this time that my eyes glazed over and I must have gone into a trance-like state of fear, because the next thing I remember was her taking the snake back off of my shoulders and putting it back in the box.

She took her bow to thunderous applause and left the stage. I'd only missed the damn show. That was the first and last time I ever had to babysit a python and got nothing for my troubles. Serves me right for trying to be one of the lads.

Here comes the bride

As the sharp-eyed readers among you will remember, I have mentioned this particular narrative on a previous page. It was while I was in the employ of Peter Macey, or the Lord, as he liked to be known.

The whole day went without a hitch, apart from the bit where we had to form a guard of honour at the church. Good lord, that was cold. One good thing about this promoter was that he would give you all the facts about the forthcoming show well in advance and I, for one, would always try and make a special effort for any one-off shows. On this occasion I had decided to enter the ring, not only as a gay boy, but one dressed in a wedding dress. It should work, I thought, as long as it didn't look tacky. So off I went to the local charity shop and purchased an old wedding dress. Kind words and a lot of explaining to a seamstress friend of mine resulted in being the proud owner of a wrestling gown shaped into a kind of dressing gown complete with a white fur collar, matching cuffs and a veil. A small train at the back, a blue garter and a bouquet completed the outfit. It might sound a bit over the top, but the reaction of the crowd as I walked down the aisle to the ring to the tune of *Here Comes The Bride* made it all worthwhile.

After I had been introduced, amid all the wolf whistles, I tossed my bouquet over my shoulder to the best man, who promptly threw it back into the ring. As a good showman should, I blew him a kiss and took off my gown. I then tantalizingly, rolled down my garter, put it down neatly folded with my gown and gave it to the second to take care of. I had plans for it later.

The bout went well and luckily, my opponent had decided, with no prompting from me, to play along. We must have performed moves that even the Kama Sutra didn't include. The crowd were loving it and took it all in good part. The bout ended in a draw (as all good marriage rows should).

After the Master of Ceremonies had given his verdict, I did something I had never done before or since. I took the microphone and called the bridegroom into the ring. Then, using a fair bit of comedy banter, I presented him with the wedding gown, complete with accessories, for his honeymoon.

It was a very enjoyable occasion all round and as we stayed for the evening party, we were made to feel very welcome by all.

Towards the end of the evening, the "Lord" took me to one side and thanked me, which is something that never happens in wrestling circles. He took out his monocle and said "Ah Jackie my boy, what an absolutely spiffing performance this afternoon, one can honestly say that you did *heveryone* proud."

"Thank you" I replied. I was thinking to myself, you really must get to grips with those aitches if you want people to really believe you're a toff.

A plague of creepy-crawlies

I don't remember the exact venue of this particular tale, but I do recall that it was a town hall on the first floor. How the ring riggers got all the equipment up those winding stairs, I will never know. They certainly earned their wages that night.

I was first on the bill, and all seemed to be going well until about the third round when we glanced down to the canvas and noticed that the ring was covered in little flies, beetles and other insects. OK, maybe not covered, but there were certainly too many to count. We carried on wrestling until the end of the round, when someone came into the ring and swept them all up. By the end of the next round there were even more creepy crawlies. What the hell was going on?

This continued, not only for the rest of the bout but through the next one as well. During the interval, an impromptu meeting was held between the promoter, the caretaker and a couple of council officials who had been called in by the caretaker. Each one took it in turns to scratch his head and come up with nothing constructive. The answer was given by one of the crowd seated at the ringside.

"They're coming from up there, mate" he said, pointing to the high ceiling.

What had happened was this. When the riggers had fixed the large lighting gantry above the ring, there was no fixing point, so they had taken the hanging chain up through a gap in the plaster and sent a rigger up into the loft area to bolt the rig to a suitable beam. In doing so, they had disturbed every insect in the loft. With the disruption to their habitat, coupled with the heat from the lighting gantry going into the loft, we had awoken the inhabitants, so we were treated to a shower of fresh insects at frequent intervals throughout the show.

Things settled down after one of the riggers returned to the loft and packed the hole with newspaper. Had it have been forty years later, I might well have shouted. "I'm a wrestler, get me out of here."

Brighton or bust

One early morning in the height of summer, several of us met up at a transport café somewhere on the outskirts of Bristol. I had been looking forward to this day for quite a while. We had been booked to appear in that lovely seaside town of Brighton and had decided to leave at the crack of dawn and hopefully spend the day at the seaside before fighting in the evening and then stay overnight before heading home the next day.

I don't remember all the details, but it had been organized by the Brighton Boys' Club as part of their fund-raising for a new clubhouse. We had our sleeping bags, as we didn't want the club to have to spend their hard-earned money on providing a hotel, as that would have defeated the object. I vaguely remember that we were doing this one free of charge except for our travelling expenses. We were doing a favour for a friend of one of the wrestlers and we would all pull together to make it as successful as possible.

We set off accompanied by my old mate Ken Banks, plus Mike and Tony Waite, the Kaeil Brothers, Bert and Gordon (real surname Higgs, but they called themselves Kaeil after Gordon had bought a car with the registration number KAE 1L) and a few others whom I have forgotten. We had hired a minibus for the trip down, with the mandatory crate of beer in the boot. After we had been travelling for about an hour the beer ran out, but not before it had worked its magic and forced us into an impromptu stop in a small forest somewhere. The Men went left, and the Ladies right. The Ladies I refer to were a mother and daughter, Dorothy and Helen Paget, who had been with us since the conception of Associated Promotions. Dorothy was a fount of knowledge about anything to do with the world of wrestling and her daughter, Helen was well known throughout the business as the best seamstress for making wrestling attire, which she did for most of the top wrestlers of the day.

Bodily functions attended to, we all piled back into the minibus and were soon on our way once more. There were a few jokes flying around and of course, the mandatory singsong, and before we knew it, the unmistakable sights of Brighton appeared and we were nearly there.

First things first. We located the hall where we were fighting that night and after a quick trip to the nearest phone box, arranged with the boys' club chairman to find out where we would be staying that night. Within a few minutes, we were confronted with the old clubhouse. We were to sleep in the part that hadn't actually fallen down yet, and just to make our stay was even more welcoming they had placed a new tarpaulin over the bit of the roof that leaked. It didn't matter, we were all younger then and it was an adventure.

Finally, we took ourselves off to the nearest café to participate in that fine old English tradition of a fry up. One hour and a few mugs of tea later, we decided to hit the town. First on our to-do list had to be the pier. Dodgems, ghost train, shooting gallery and trips up and down on the little train, you name it, we did it. We finally left the pier with the usual arms full of cuddly toys and a kiss-me-quick hat each. Next came the stroll on the sands, culminating in a friendly argument with the man on the donkey rides over the suggestion that we were too old. Ice creams, candy floss, a few beers in the pub and the knowledge that in a few hours' time we were going to be bounced around the ring made us all feel sick, so we did the decent thing and headed for the deck chairs. We knew in the backs of our minds that in two hours' time we needed to get back to the hall and put up the ring, no mean feat given the way that we had abused our digestive systems. However, we were all professionals and we did what was needed in plenty of time, which meant that we could just relax for the next two hours. I say relax - there was Gordon moaning because he felt sick and our Master of Ceremonies, Pete Jollife, complaining that he had caught the sun on his back after falling asleep on the beach, but on the whole, we were a pretty intact bunch.

The wrestling went well and we had a full house with people standing at the back. We managed to raise a tidy sum, much to the delight of the club members. At the end we were all invited back into the ring to be thanked and congratulated by the local Mayor, who was so delighted at our efforts that he gave poor old Pete Joliffe a hearty slap on the back. His eyes filled with water and he choked out a 'thank you'. The Mayor assumed Pete had found the moment unexpectedly moving, but we knew it was sunburn.

It was decided earlier in the day that we should have a whip round and put the two ladies into a hotel for the night, as the place where we were staying was, to say the least, a bit basic. A taxi was ordered to take them to their beds while the rest of us took down the ring, put the chairs away and generally tidied up. After a quick drink on our way to the clubhouse, we were ready for a long-awaited sleep.

It was not the best night's sleep I had ever had, as I recall. The rain threw it down onto the tin roof and tarpaulin, and our daytime activities with our digestive systems came back to haunt us with a vengeance. Needless to say, most of us were grateful when the morning came. A bucket of tepid water saw to our ablution needs and we bid a fond farewell to Brighton.

The trip back home was uneventful - no singing, no beer and hardly any conversation. All you could hear was the odd groan and the occasional noise of a Rennie being sucked. I remember thinking that this whole episode had many similarities to that wonderful film *Carry On At Your Convenience*.

The customer is always wrong

As mentioned in the previous tale, the subject of staying in digs deserves a mention (see next chapter). In fact it could well be a book of its own. As anyone who has travelled for long periods on the road will tell you, it is a different world out there.

In the early days of my career when shillings were hard to come by, I found myself staying overnight as cheaply as possible. I have already mentioned that I spent a couple of seasons in my fairground days living in a caravan with two strippers and a bearded lady. Believe it or not, it was going to get a lot worse.

It was somewhere in mid Wales when I discovered that I couldn't find suitable digs for the night and as a last resort, I made enquiries at the local police station. "Old Beatty up at the farm lets out rooms for the night, doesn't she?" the desk sergeant enquired from his colleagues.

"That's right, she does. Just go to the top of the lane opposite, sir, you can't miss it. It's through a big wooden gate."

I thanked them and set out. Time was getting short and it was only an hour before I needed to be at the venue. The winter night was setting in and it was already dark. I found the place easily enough and banged on the big old heavy farm door. It was answered by a big old heavy farmer's wife, who ushered me into a typical farm kitchen. On enquiring, I was issued with a key to my room for the night. It was to my delight a pleasant room with all the amenities that would be required for a good night's stay.

There was a knock on the door - the lady of the house, bringing me fresh towels. She pointed out that the bathroom and toilet were just down the landing and enquired as to my business in this area. I informed her that I was appearing at the town hall that night.

"How wonderful" she replied, and informed me that her and her sister were going to see it. "We never miss it," she said. "Now would you like a nice cup of tea before you leave?" I thanked her very much and made my way down to the warmth of the kitchen.

Two cups of tea later I left for the town hall. I don't remember much of the evening, it was a normal, run-of-the-mill type of show and everyone seemed happy with their lot. I had a quick natter and catch up with the wrestlers I hadn't seen for a while and finally made my way back to the farm. When I arrived I noticed that the kitchen light was still on. Good, I thought, I might get a cup of tea before I turn in.

As soon as I had let myself in and closed the door behind me, it started. I turned to find the two sisters standing there in their candlewick dressing gowns and hairnets, glowering at me.

"You dirty swine!" said one.

"How can you show your face here?" said the sister.

"Pardon?" I replied.

"You were punching him behind the ref's back, we saw you. Huh, you can't win a fight properly so you have to resort to cheating."

This went on for a few minutes and all I could do was to stand there open-mouthed at this tirade of abuse. "Ladies, it was just a bit of entertainment" I replied. "Huh, is that what you call it?" And so it went on.

I tried my best to calm things down, but finally I gave it up and went to bed. The next morning at breakfast was no better. My tea was banged down in front of me and my breakfast was practically thrown at me. I looked across at the two other guests who had been staying and threw an embarrassed smile in their direction.

"Don't worry," said the young man, once he had checked that the ladies had left the room and the coast was clear, "we've heard all about it this morning. I nodded a quick thank you and finished my breakfast. Luckily for me, I always make a point of paying for my digs as soon as I arrive in case a fight goes wrong and I am taken to hospital. If that should ever happen then at least my hosts are never out of pocket."

So after breakfast I made a quick but silent departure, having left a note thanking them for a very interesting stay.

They picked the wrong party

I and several of my fellow fighters had received an invitation to attend a function at a smart hotel in the vicinity of Chesterfield, which had been organized by a popular health and fitness magazine of the day. I guess it was something to do with an article that was running, or maybe an advertising campaign. It didn't really matter, it sounded good. Why Chesterfield? That fine Peak District town was a good place for me as my father was born and brought up in the little village of Shirebrook, near Mansfield, so that whole area held lots of childhood memories for me.

That weekend was a very pleasant experience and apart from the regimented itinerary we were faced with, which is expected when a trip is organized by a magazine, the weekend was a time for relaxing, comparing notes and making new friends and contacts. There was a plethora of people from all kinds of sports and martial arts clubs, weightlifters, judo experts and prizefighters from right across the land were all present, as well as the usual dignitaries. We sat down to a grand meal and listened to speeches and presentations from various quarters and generally enjoyed the hospitality on offer. The evening culminated in entertainment from a local band in the entertainment marquee set in the grounds of the hotel.

Everything was going well until about eleven thirty, when about fifteen of the local Hell's Angels fraternity decided it would be a good idea to gatecrash the party. They must have thought it was a wedding reception or something. Can you imagine their shock at finding out that the bloke they thought was the best man was, in reality, the world champion Kung Fu exponent, who wasn't happy being pushed in the back and spilling his mineral water over his best suit. I will not go into detail of what happened next, but when the police arrived to find that the party was in full swing and there appeared to be nothing wrong, they were somewhat surprised.

"That's OK, officer. We've put them outside on the lawn in two heaps" I said. "The ones on the left need to go to hospital, you can do what you like with the others."

Police vans were ordered and the troublemakers were taken away. We heard nothing more about it, but can you imagine what would have happened in this day? There would have been lawsuits flying about everywhere, police would have arrested practically everybody, compensation claims by the dozen would have been filed. But life was much simpler then.

Looking back over some of my stories, there always seems to be a common thread of humour running throughout. It would be wrong of me to portray the life of a wrestler through rose-tinted spectacles, when, in fact, it was like any other job. It had an enjoyable side, of course, but with that, came the inevitable problems, disappointments and frustrations of any occupation. I was and still am a strong advocate of looking on the bright side and pride myself on looking for good in people wherever possible.

That aside, there have been times in my career where I have actually feared for my life. In most cases this has been at the hands of an over-zealous fan, or a group of people I have inadvertently upset by my antics in the ring. I have said before that I chose to be a 'dirty' fighter, partly as this went with the persona I had developed, but to be honest, I wasn't a skilled enough wrestler to make it without being a baddie.

Eventually, I became better and more skilful at my job as the time went on but by then, the die was cast and most of my work came because I was able to put bums on seats. My living depended on it, so I had no choice.

Come on girls, straighten me out

My wrestling persona, playing as a gay boy, had several drawbacks, especially in the early days when I had to fight another wrestler who didn't know much about me. They would have many reservations about it (I would have too, in their position). Many of them would tell me of their initial fears, once they had got to know me a bit better and realised that I was just one of the lads. They thought it would be like wrestling a girl, and were waiting for me to burst into tears if they so much as smudged my lipstick. In some cases, they thought I might make sexual advances towards them in the ring. I took all this as a compliment. If I could convince them that easily that I was gay, I must be doing a good job as far as the audiences were concerned.

It very soon came to light that I had convinced the audience, not only by the stick I was given by the male contingent, which I thought in itself was a drawback but by the fact that some of them treated me as a freak.

There were however several advantages for a young lad of my age who played his gay persona to the limit, and that was the number of ladies who not only wanted to mother me but would buy me gifts of make-up and other things of that nature. The best thing was that many of them wanted to "straighten me out", as they put it. So being a young lad at the time, I would let them try. You would be surprised at how many of them claimed they were the one who turned me back into a man again. Oh well, boys will be boys and it was all good fun.

That is, until I came across Bertha. That wasn't her name of course, as I never got close enough to find out her real name, but that was what all the other wrestlers would call her, as they tried their hardest to set me up on many occasions

Bertha, who was probably a very nice person, would wait for me outside the changing rooms at various venues within travelling distance of her home, eager to get me in her grasp and show me exactly what she thought I was missing. It wasn't long before I became intimate friends with every fire escape in most of the halls in that area. To give you some idea of what I was up against, she made the bearded lady from my fairground wrestling days, look like Doris Day. I would have nightmares of finding myself in her clutches and wake up in a hot sweat.

It didn't last though. Eventually she stopped coming to the wrestling and nothing more was heard of her. I like to think that she found herself a boyfriend and settled down somewhere to live a pleasant and contented life, and that she made him very happy, whoever the poor sod was.

Grilled by the Inquisition

From time to time I would get a request to do a talk on wrestling from youth clubs, sports clubs and a variety of other bodies, aiming to make money for a charity or finance some sort of improvements to their own facilities.

On one occasion I was asked to talk to a local Women's Institute. The usual format on these occasions was to talk generally about my job for 30 minutes and then to spend a further 30 minutes answering any questions. This particular evening would be a breeze, or so I thought. I was sure I would be asked things like how often I laddered my tights, what brand of make-up I used and similar questions which would require easy answers.

I could not have been more wrong. They grilled me practically the whole time I was there, barely giving me time to take a breath. "Why on earth would someone who seemed to be such a reasonable person feel the need to fight anyone for the sake of earning money?" said one. I responded in the best way I thought appropriate by saying it was something I had wanted to do from about the age of eight. So was it something to do with a violent childhood? I responded, "Not at all, I had a perfectly normal upbringing as far as I was concerned." Was I bullied at school, they wanted to know? No, I was not bullied at school. What I didn't add was, "Because none of you were in my class, thank goodness."

Then came what seemed like a kind act from one dear old lady; a normal question was asked. "Considering the amount of travelling you have to do, is it financially worthwhile?"

"I earn enough for my needs."

"So the spoils are good then?"

"I am a wrestler, not a grade A villain."

"Of course you're not, but we are trying to understand what the difference is." Then I had to open my big mouth. "The same difference as that between the Women's Institute and the Gestapo, I should think."

Lamb to the slaughter comes to mind. It was the

longest 30 minutes of my life. Give me eight rounds with a 30-stone wrestler any day. By the end of this interrogation, I was a gibbering wreck.

I was brought another cup of tea, as the next stage of the evening was to gently sip your tea whilst generally chatting to the audience, having once left the stage. Oh my god, I thought, they are throwing me to the wolves. I was wrong again; they were all perfectly charming. What was happening here? A few minutes ago they were verbally tearing me limb from limb. I happened to mention the change of attitude to one senior lady, once I had established that the question wasn't likely to get me my face torn off. She informed me that having been given the details of the speaker a few days before, they had set out to research their subject and ask the sort of questions that would impress their fellow members.

"It's a case of being one up on the others with these ladies" she said. "It's nothing personal. Anyway, we are always calmer after the tea has arrived."

At the end of the evening, the leader of the pack took to the stage and thanked me very much for such an interesting and enjoyable discussion and, to my surprise I received a round of applause.

I must admit that my departure from that living hell was as fast as I could possibly make it. Never again would I talk again at any function that sported the initials WI.

Posing for the posters

I just loved making them suffer

The body slam

Jackie (Glitterboy) Evans

Honest ref, it was the flat of the hand

Never kick a man when he's down - unless you are the Glitterboy

Slammed into the corner post

Always time for autographs

Tag match at Brockworth Fete

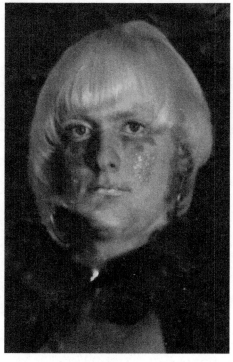

My Glam Rock period

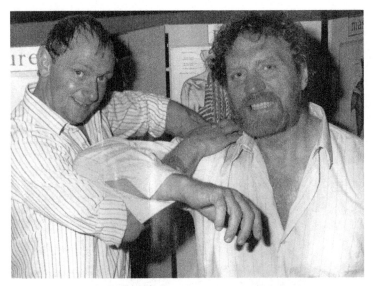

The author with wrestler and actor Pat 'Bomber' Roach
(by kind permission of the Andover Advertiser)

Always ready to share a joke with every wrestler's friend,
Johnny Kincaid, one of the best wrestlers ever

Spending time with the former British middleweight and,
welterweight champion, Brian 'Goldbelt' Maxine

With Jackie Pallo Junior, son of the great Jackie 'Mr TV' Pallo

With former world heavyweight champion Wayne Bridges

The author

Landladies from hell

There was nothing more formidable in those days than a Blackpool landlady, especially to those of us who were known as 'theatricals'. The breakfast table would always be of particular interest. A big sign on the wall would give a list of dining room rules, no muddy boots, please ask if you need the use of the cruet and no Marmite provided.

This particular hovel was under the control, with a rod of iron, of a Mrs Priddy, whose particular party piece was to serve breakfast dressed in a dark blue candlewick dressing gown, complete with hairnet. Luckily for me, there were three builders staying there for the duration of the job in hand, and they were to take the brunt of Mrs Priddy. I was to be a mere bystander, so I could sit back and enjoy the friction between them. Three builders versus Mrs Priddy? My money was on her.

The conversation went something like this:

Builder 1: "Any chance of a bit more toast here luv?"

Mrs P: "Oi you, less of the luv. You'll have to wait, I'm busy."

Builder 2: "Where's Mr Priddy today, still keeping him chained up in the yard then?"

Mrs P: "Don't you be so cheeky, or you'll feel the back of my hand young man. Shouldn't you be at work by now?"

Builder 3: "Nah, too wet today, been rained off."

Mrs P: "Well you're not hanging round here all day, I got my cleaning to do, and I'm not doing lunches."

Builder 1: "We're not asking you too missus."

Mrs P: "Don't you talk to me like that you cheeky bugger, I'll slap your face."

And so it went on. I was mesmerized and somewhat surprised at the builders for their backchat. They deserved some serious respect. I had stood up to some serious opponents in my time, but nothing like Mrs Priddy.

All went well for me until she happened to catch me smiling at one of the comments given by Builder 2. Then it was my turn.

"Don't you dare encourage them, you're as bad, expecting me to be running around looking after you, damn theatricals, you're all the same. And what time did you get in last night? You made enough noise."

I sat there open-mouthed, not daring to speak. Meanwhile, the builders had quietly left the dining room. Cheers chaps, I thought, you've dropped me right in it. I did the decent thing and apologized as I beat a hasty retreat to my room.

I left the digs at around ten o' clock that morning, knowing enough about digs to realise that if you were a few minutes late in vacating your room you would have to spend two hours on the rack in the cellar (or so I believed.) The day was my own until about four o clock, when I would have to leave. I decided to have a look around the sights of Blackpool and around lunchtime, I popped into a greasy spoon café for lunch. Who did I see sitting at a table at the far end of the café but the three builders from the breakfast fiasco.

"I hope we didn't drop you in it this morning," sniggered one.

"Nothing I couldn't handle" I replied sarcastically. I ordered my lunch and nothing more was said.

The owner of this particular establishment was a somewhat morose man of about thirty stone in weight and big with it. He didn't seem to be the sort of man you could have a joke with, or indeed, would take kindly to anyone criticizing his running of such a dog hole. Past experience had taught me that in those kinds of places, the cook would take pride in their cuisine and woe betide anyone who didn't appreciate their efforts.

It was for this reason that I decided I would have a

word in his ear, on my way out. "Excuse me," I said, "I would just like to say that I thoroughly enjoyed my meal and although those builder blokes over there told me your chips were disgusting, I found them lovely."

I made my exit, turning around at the door in time to see the owner of the café making his way over to the three builders.

Out of the toilet window

Another worrying episode in my career, and perhaps potentially more dangerous than anything before, was the night I went to Cardiff Arms Park. This was one of those occasions which had been especially organized by a private group or association in order to raise much-needed cash for something we were not privy to, but as a properly contracted booking, we would turn up, do our job and wish them all the best with their endeavour.

For those who have never been to this particular sporting venue, I will say that it has long been the home of Welsh rugby. It was a massive place and very impressive, and the pitch seemed to go on and on into the distance. The wrestling ring looked as though someone had dropped it on the grass and not noticed it was missing, it looked so small. The promoter gathered us together before the start and formulated a plan of action as to how we were going to master that long walk to the ringside and back again afterwards. We decided that two open-backed vehicles would be the best idea and so it was arranged.

The evening got under way in front of the biggest crowd I have ever seen. It was just a sea of people all cheering and shouting. I was on in the third bout with a lad I had never met before. I was soon to learn that he came from Cardiff and was hailed as the local hero among the Welsh wrestling fans. A nice bloke, as I recall. We chatted for a while about the people in the business, that we knew, swapped the odd tale between us and generally relaxed in each other's company.

Eventually, our turn came and we left to get the transport to the ringside. The fight went as well as could be expected and by the end and true to form, I got disqualified. Nothing unusual about that, I thought, the crowd was cheering their lad and booing me and so I left the ring. To say that it was a nightmare journey back to the dressing room was an understatement. Twice the vehicle had to pull up suddenly so as not to hit the angry crowd that had gathered, baying for my blood, and each time, had it not been for the skill of my driver they would have tipped the thing over.

Eventually, I reached the safety of the security gate and in no time at all I was ushered back to the dressing room by four burly security guards. It didn't end there though, because when the last bout was finished there came a hammering on the changing-room door as half a dozen great big rugby players attempted to get at me.

"Quick, this way" called my earlier opponent, beckoning me to the toilet block. I soon realised what he meant and started to climb out of the small toilet window. "I'll meet you round the back" he said, and he was gone. By this time the other wrestlers had thrown their weight behind the main door, which apparently was about to lose its hinges as I disappeared from sight.

I was outside the open window wondering what to do next when a car sped round the corner and the familiar voice of my opponent shouted, "Get in!" I leapt into the back seat and away we sped. After a few minutes, once we were clear of the venue, he slowed the car to a more gentle speed and muttered, "That was close".

"How did you get out?" I asked.

"Oh I went down the fire escape. It's a good job you didn't follow me, three of them were waiting there as well."

"What was that all about?" I said. He just laughed and said in an exaggerated Welsh accent "Never underestimate the power and feelings of a Welsh sports fan, boyo." I laughed out loud, more out of relief that anything else.

It was a good hour before we dared to venture back into the stadium, having made sure that the coast was clear. Apart from a few security and cleaners, the place was deserted. I duly picked up my wages, thanked the promoter and with a wry smile told him not to ring me and that I would ring him if ever I felt like topping myself. I shook hands with my opponent and eventual savior of the day and took my leave. It was a long drive home that night and every car that came up behind me was, in my irrational state of mind, a hit man. I eventually got over that particular event and was to spend many enjoyable nights of wrestling in many different parts of Wales, but that night will stay with me for the rest of my life.

Hi de hi!

Most of the fights and venues would turn out to be much the same to me. Turn up, do your stuff, then off to the next one and so it went on. But now and then, a contract would come up which would be a whole new ball game, such as was when I was asked if I would be interested in doing what was known in the business as the Butlin's circuit. I jumped at it of course. It was to be a total contrast to what I was used to. In those days there were a dozen or so different camps dotted all over the country, and though this would mean a fair bit of travelling around from one camp to the other, it did have its better side. Sleeping arrangements were laid on, as was the food aspect. At that time in the early seventies, wrestling was reaching its peak, so there would be plenty of people to cheer you on (or in my case, to boo you off). If time allowed, you could take advantage of the entertainment and general fun and games that these places so generously provided. No having to put up and dismantle the ring, as each camp had its own designated arena. Oh, it was going to be wonderful.

The season ran for about four months (now the camps that are left open all year round). I could stand the four months of summer doing this, I had no doubt.

The season came round quick enough and before we knew it, we were off. It took a while to work out the best routes to travel, but once that was under control it was good fun.

The biggest worry with any promoter is to put on a good all-round show of wrestling, never placing wrestlers together in any one venue too often and certainly not in consecutive visits. With this circuit it was different. By the time we had been around all the camps and got back to where we started, the campers had gone home and a fresh lot had arrived, so it didn't matter who you were fighting. In fact, at one point, I fought the same wrestler six nights a week for months. By the end of it, we each knew what the other was thinking, never mind the moves.

I always looked forward to the Minehead camp best as I was able to spend more leisure time there, because the next day we were in Barry Island and that was probably the shortest journey between any of the camps. Just a couple of hours would do it. As a rule, if we had long distances to travel we would travel overnight as the roads were quieter, but Minehead was as near to a day off as we were likely to get. Except for Sundays, which usually ended up being a home day if you were married, or a launderette day if you were not.

We would arrive at Minehead after driving from Skegness at about six in the morning, check into our chalet and then go for breakfast, then sleep for a few hours until lunchtime. Then you had to fight twice, once for the second sitting for dinner and again for the first. It seemed a strange way to do it, but I suppose they had their reasons. Once the two fights were out of the way, the rest of the day and night were our own. Although I have never been a drinker (in fact, I have always been happier with a cup of tea), it did mean we could have a few beers, as we were not driving until the next day. This was my chance of getting in a bit of swimming and the odd game of snooker. Yes, Minehead was my favourite.

That does not mean that the other camps were any the less inviting, they all had their good points. The food always seemed better at Filey and the tea better at Clacton. I've no doubt that it was all in the mind, but nevertheless that was my impression.

The audiences at the holiday camps were always good ones, probably because they did not have to buy tickets weeks in advance. There were, of course, the regulars - by this, I mean the ones who followed wrestling to the full and could reel off stuff about the game that I'd never heard of. They could tell you who had fought, who, and who had won, how many submissions and pinfalls had been given, how many public warnings. You would see them at four o'clock on the Saturday, glued to the televisions in the lounges, shouting and booing. Bless them all, because those were the ones who helped pay my wages.

Then there would be those campers who had never been to a wrestling match in their lives but would venture in out of curiosity. Some would stay for a few minutes, raise their eyebrows and leave, while others were hooked from the start. The main reason for the ever-rising interest in wrestling was of course television, but I would like to think that we at the holiday camps had made a small contribution.

Not only did I have a great time at the camps that season but I returned a year later for another four-month stint. As memories go, the hospitality shown by Mr Billy Butlin and his staff at all the camps will always stay with me.

Blood is thicker than water

Over the years when I'm asked about wrestling there are certain questions people always want to ask you. Of course, the first one is always "Is it fixed?" (I have answered this one in a previous chapter - no). The second is usually "do you get hurt?" and the answer is always yes. It stands to reason that given the nature of the game, it is bound to happen. Most wrestlers in my day would be willing to help you if you had a shoulder joint pop out, they would hold your shoulder with one hand and pull your arm out and slot it back in. It would be sore for a few days but it would do the trick.

I have even put my own back in by putting my arm around the corner post, holding my wrist with the other hand and pulling until I felt it drop back into place. (It wouldn't be allowed today, not without the right certificate on your wall, Health and Safety would be all over you.) We also carried a needle and cotton so that if we had a cut, we would put in our own stiches. Don't get me wrong, it wasn't bravado, it was a case of not wanting to spend hours waiting in the nearest casualty department late at night when you should be travelling to your next booking.

Injuries were fairly common among wrestlers, but injuries to a member of the audience were a whole new ball game. As I remember, it didn't happen often but when it did, it got messy.

I remember one particular evening, I believe in Shepton Mallet in Somerset. I had finished for the night, showered and changed and was standing at the back of the hall, watching the last bout. I don't remember the exact line up, but one of the fighters was a great friend of mine from Yate, Bristol called Maurice Dracup. I had known Maurice from the early days in the ring and he would also be the last fight I would have, as a professional (more of that later). This night, both fighters came out of the ring, taking the referee with them, and in the mayhem, a lady in the front row received a small cut to the leg. The Red Cross man managed to stop the bleeding and put a plaster over the cut, and we thought that was that. The lady herself seemed OK about it, but her son had decided that he was going to take it further.

At the end of the evening when the crowd had drifted away, the police were called and we were all asked to stay and make statements. Most of us realised that it was something about nothing, and even the police hinted to that effect, but still the man insisted, so statements were taken. The lady by this time was totally embarrassed by the whole episode and just wanted to go home, but her son was having none of it. Not only did he want all the wrestlers publicly flogged in the street and thrown into prison, he wanted the Government brought down as well.

Maurice, who was a great guy but not known for his diplomacy, suggested "Why don't I just smack him in the gob, then we can all go home?" Good old Maurice, he did make me laugh, but, eventually he did save the day. He stood in front of the lady and knelt down, took her hand, stared earnestly into her eyes and said softly, "You enjoyed the wrestling, didn't you?" She nodded. "In fact you got quite excited, didn't you?" "Yes" she uttered. "When you got excited, you picked a scab off your leg, didn't you?"

By this time, we all knew where he was going with this, including the lady, who just wanted to go home.

"Yes that's exactly what happened" she said. Then she turned to her son "and if you don't like it Raymond that's tough, now stop being so bloody stupid and let's go home." She was happy, the police were happy and so were we.

I often wonder what ever happened to Maurice over the years. The last I heard of him, he had a plant hire business in Yate. No doubt, still as charming as ever.

How to knock out a helicopter

I cannot write this book without mentioning the many charity fetes we were called upon to do. They were a law unto themselves. Not only did we find ourselves fighting in the rain and have difficulty standing up on a slippery canvas, let alone fight, we also had quite a walk to and from the ring. Even then, we would be bombarded with ice creams, beer cans, and a variety of items from the bric-a-brac stall. They were generally regarded by us as an inconvenience, but at the same time, it was a day out (that is, if you didn't have to fight somewhere else that night). Once in a while you would have the ring put up in a good-size marquee, but in most cases the coffers didn't run to it so you were out in the open, and if you were near the coast, you kept an eye out for messy seagulls.

I remember one such event; I was fighting a wrestler by the name of Jim Mager. A nice, amiable bloke who should, in my opinion, have reached a higher rating in the game than he did. For some reason, the wrestling had started at two, the same time as a model helicopter flying display in the main arena. Wrestling being what it was, we attracted most of the crowd and the arena area was practically empty, much to the annoyance of the display team. One of the flyers decided that it was time to act, so he started to fly his model helicopter over the ring, making it hover a few feet above our heads. The first bout came off complaining that the organizers should sort it out, but Jim just said "don't worry lads, leave it to me." We all knew him well enough to know that if he said it, it would be sorted.

Sure enough, we had been fighting for a few minutes when over came the helicopter and started to hover. What followed was probably the best and most original wrestling move I have ever seen. I had Jim in a full nelson (my arms under his, with my hands clasped behind his head). He grabbed my hands, pushed them away, ran to the corner post, ran up the post, flipped upside down in the air, kicked the helicopter out of the sky, landed behind me and got me in a full nelson. The crowd erupted, all except the gentleman (I am very reluctant to call him an anorak) who came over to retrieve his bits of helicopter. He did however hang about long enough to confront Jim as he got out of the ring. Jim, towering over him, whispered, gently to him, "If you don't go away little man, I will run up your trouser leg and do the same to your teeth." Needless to say, he left.

On the whole, appearing at a fete was a good experience and there were always many autographs to sign as well as being well looked after and generally mothered by the WI ladies on the cake stalls.

Encounter with a hero

I was fast approaching the halfway mark in my career when one day a booking came in for work in a small town in Somerset. It came with a note attached, which said, "Dear Jackie, can you do this one? It should be an interesting night as, apparently, Jackie Pallo is on the bill". Never, I thought, not in a million years. The legendary Pallo would not be interested in a small venue like this (small by his standards, anyway). He was one of the top men at Dale Martin, the ones who had more franchise than all the others put together. I couldn't see that being true. Nevertheless, I took it, as I wasn't booked that night anyway. And true to form, the first person I bumped into that night was the great man himself.

We chatted for a while over coffee, him rambling on about the lovely countryside he had driven through on his way down and me pinching myself under the table to make sure I wasn't dreaming. (I know, sad isn't it), but he had been one of my childhood heroes, and here I was, sitting here talking to him.

"How's things at the top?" I said, instantly realising what a stupid thing I had just said. He smiled and put his cup down and in a serious moment replied, "I wasn't born there you know, I had to claw my way up the ladder the same as everyone." I nodded a sort of apology. He continued, "You'll get there one day, I've heard of you before and I reckon that the next time you and I take a coffee together will be at a Dale Martin production, and by the way, it will be my turn to buy the coffee." He smiled, got up and left.

I often sit and think of that moment and wonder whether he had really heard of me or he was just being polite. I would never know. I didn't really mind. I had shared a chat with the great Jackie "Mr TV" Pallo and that was all that mattered.

The evening went well and of course it was a packed audience. At the end of his bout, Jackie Pallo stood up in the ring and announced to everyone that he had really enjoyed the evening and that it was his intention to appear in all the wrestling halls across England before he finally "hung up his boots". True to form, he kept his promise and I saw him many times after that. He of course, shared a smile and a passing nod, but it would be a few years until I spoke with him again and more importantly, many more years on top of that before he finally did "hang up his boots."

Fish and ships

Many weeks later I had a booking to appear at a venue somewhere in North Wales. I remember the venue well, as by night it was used for all forms of entertainment but by day it was a fish market. Interesting, I thought, smelly but interesting. I must say at this point that I had been in the game long enough not to bother with looking at posters to see who I was fighting or who I was on the bill with. It might sound a bit high and mighty, but all that interested me was the directions and the name of the venue.

Judging by the time it took to get there and the amount of times I got lost, this venue was not too well known. Eventually I arrived and managed to find the dressing room, which consisted of a large piece of muslin draped over a steel girder in the corner of the massive area and in between the lines of fish barrows all around the edge. Not only was it cramped, it was freezing cold. I remember thinking that if it didn't warm up, I would be going in the ring with my coat on.

I was bent down putting my boots on when all of a sudden I felt a sharp slap on my backside and a familiar voice shouted "Hey up Jacks, how are ya doing?"

I didn't need to look; I knew that voice anywhere and there was only one person who ever called me Jacks. "How's it going, Ada?" I replied. It was Adrian Street. I'd met him several times on my travels and after my initial concern that he would be annoyed at me for working the same gimmick as him, we got on OK. I had indeed chosen my persona on the back of his, but more out of respect than anything else. He didn't seem to mind that and secretly I think he was the tiniest bit flattered.

The promoter came in at that stage and enquired if everything was OK. "It's a bit chilly" one chap said.

"Ah, you English, are you men or mice, up here we call it bracing."

"Are there any showers?" asked another.

"I'll sort you out, don't worry." said the boss. "We have more to worry about than that, anyway. We've got two poofs on the bill tonight and that's one poof too many, so one of you will have to be a proper man tonight."

I thought Ada was going to punch him. However I decided that I would play it straight as most, if not all, the crowd had come to see him, as he was a well-known fighter and popular with audiences all over the country. The promoter, his aggravating attitude aside, was right, and although we were not fighting each other it would not have been right.

The evening went its usual way with the crowd seeming to enjoy it, but it was quieter than usual, probably due to the shouting and booing being filtered out by heavy muffler's and scarves as everyone, including us, froze to death.

True to his word, the promoter had provided us with a shower - well not exactly a shower, it was a big bucket of cold water on a table. It didn't really matter much as it was so cold that we didn't really work up much of a sweat and anyway, I could take a shower when I got back to the digs. I just managed to splash my face a bit and prayed that it wouldn't all end in cold sores. The promoter was no help. "Would you like some ice with that?" he said, laughing as he passed. I must remember not to work for him in the future, I thought. A thought I retracted when he paid us an extra twenty pounds each because of the conditions.

We finished in good time, all the audience had left and we were ready to make a move. "What is it tonight lads?" said one of the wrestlers, "Indian or Chinese?"

"You must be joking," I said, "this place can't even provide a town hall so it's hardly likely to have a restaurant."

"It's got a chip shop," said the voice of the caretaker, from somewhere behind us.

"Forget it," I said, "I've had enough of fish for one night."

Mr Bigmouth

It doesn't matter what industry you find yourself in or in what group of workmates you have around you, there is always one who takes great pleasure in throwing his weight around, mouthing off and generally irritating the whole group. Wrestling is no different. His name was

Lewis and he was hell bent on making himself important and not caring whom he trampled on for his own ends.

"I've had enough of this Lewis bloke" said Paddy, a wrestler who originated from
Ireland. "He needs taking down a peg."

"Just ignore him" I advised.

"Easier said than done" he replied. "Someone needs to sort him out."

A few weeks later we were presented with an opportunity. One of the lads was due to go to London headquarters to sign a new contract, so he promised to make a few discreet enquiries about this Lewis chap. We knew little about him apart from the fact that he owned a high-class restaurant in Leeds City Centre.

A week later, I had an excited telephone call from Paddy, informing me that he now had the address of this restaurant and as I was fighting near there in a few days' time, would I be able to come up a day early with the rest of the lads on the bill so that we could have a meal at this establishment and see if we could get something on this Lewis to put him in his place? What was Paddy up to, I wondered? He obviously knew more than he was telling.

The evening soon came round and nine of us were standing outside the restaurant. To give Lewis his due, it looked a posh affair and the menu on the wall outside proved it.

"Right lads, this is the place" said Paddy, smiling to himself.

"Hang on a minute Paddy. You're not expecting us to take it apart, are you?" said one chap.

"Good lord no" he replied. "But I've been doing a bit of digging and it seems he doesn't own it. He's only the waiter, or one of them anyway, so we are just going to cause him embarrassment of the first degree. God knows, he deserves it."

Not one of us could disagree with that so in we went. Wouldn't you know it - it was one of his nights off. We did however have a great meal and an enjoyable evening and managed to talk to various members of the staff and tell them why we had come. None of them seemed surprised, as he had given them the impression that he was the owner of the promotions business we all worked for. The evening ended with the manager buying us all a drink and promising that they would all rag him their end if we would do the same at our end.

Boy, did he go through the mangle over the next few months. It did however calm him down, and apart from the odd time when he vented his supremacy, only to be knocked down to the level of the rest of us, he never pushed his luck again.

Voices from heaven

Even the best-laid plans can go awry, as we all know.

One night I turned up at a venue that had been on my books for a couple of weeks only to find that there had been a mix up and I wasn't on the bill. After a discussion with the boss and getting confirmation that I was not at fault and therefore would be paid, I took myself off for an evening on the town. After about an hour of searching, the only thing I could get tickets for was an evening of song by the Treorchy Male Voice Choir, who were performing at a nearby theatre. Oh well, I thought, better than sitting in a hotel on my own, so in I went.

That was definitely a turning point in my musical taste, because they were fantastic. To hear a hundred Welshmen singing their hearts out about their homeland with such pride and conviction was inspiring. So much so that over the years, I must have heard them live over thirty times and have proudly travelled miles to do so. I still do, to this day.

During the interval I popped outside to get a bit of fresh air, as in those days it was permitted to smoke in such venues and it soon filled up with a blue haze. I was lucky enough to see many of the choir outside as well and chatted to them like old friends. Each one had a beer in one hand and a pipe or cigarette in the other.

"My god" I said to one of them "Doesn't smoking ruin your voices?" I realised as soon as I said it that this wasn't the first time they had heard it.

"We all enjoy our singing, it's a great night out for us" said one chap. "And it includes a beer or two and a smoke if we want one." I nodded my approval. "Yes, forgive me, I didn't think." They all readily accepted my apology.

Many times since that night, when I have been lucky enough to be in their company, I have nipped out during the interval for a beer and a natter with the greatest bunch of talented lads you could ever wish to meet. I don't go out much nowadays but I'm always willing to travel miles to spend the evening in the company of the Treorchy Male Voice Choir, who have become affectionately known in our family as The Boys.

Bye bye baby

It was the early hours of the morning, and a few of us found ourselves sitting in a transport café somewhere in the Midlands. We were on our way from somewhere in Scotland and travelling down to the West Country to be there ready to fight that night. We had a big greasy breakfast and a few cups of tea inside us, and we were taking a moment to relax and chat before hitting the road and continuing our journey.

We heard a slight commotion at the counter and turned to see what was happening - human nature I guess. There was quite a bit of bad language from a group of lads, all aimed at the lady who was serving. "I'm not having that," said one of my mates, and he rose from his chair and went to remonstrate with them. To cut a long story short, the place erupted and the foul-mouthed lads were silenced.

I have to add that, on the whole, wrestlers are not fighters by nature and would generally shy away from any form of confrontation, especially as they are not getting paid for it. However, as many of us would agree, even to this day, swearing in public, and especially at a lady, is a big NO.

The police were called and verbal statements were taken. It was during this that we discovered that the thugs were associates of the pop group the Bay City Rollers. We were not sure how many of them were actual band members, if any, but there were many of their entourage, crew or roadies, and such like. I remember thinking, what's the point of wearing your tartan scarf around your waist on a cold night like this, which was the fashion of the band at that time?. But what do I know, I was even a dinosaur in those days.

The police indicated that common sense should prevail, and apart from their initial report, no action was to be taken.

This didn't seem to satisfy a couple of the roadies, who piped up, "Huh, that's not good enough, we are with the Bay City Rollers pop group and demand that these tough thugs are arrested." The policeman put his notebook into his top pocket and sauntered over to them, saying, "I've heard them singing, that should be a criminal offence straight away." We stifled a laugh, mainly because we didn't want to kick it all off again, and anyway, we needed to get back on the road. We never heard anything further on the matter and put it down to occupational hazard.

We made our next booking in plenty of time, with a few hours' sleep at the other end. No one the worse for our previous adventure, I just hope that the Bay City Rollers, suffered no time loss and went on to entertain their audiences, wherever they were heading.

The demise of a legend

It is with a somewhat saddened heart that I tell you of my next story, as it serves as a reminder of what a tightrope we and people like us walk every day of our chosen career. There but for the grace of God, and all that stuff.

I was wrestling somewhere in the Midlands and was about to reach what I thought would be a milestone in the world of wrestling. I will mention no name, but suffice to say that I was about to wrestle a man who had been one of my childhood heroes, and over the years I had come to greatly respect him. There had been many of them of course but this gentleman, without a doubt, was among the top ten. We were called to the ring as usual, and I took up my place in the blue corner with my opponent in the red corner. We were introduced by the Master of Ceremonies and awaited the bell for the first round.

Earlier that evening, in the changing rooms, I had

noticed that this great man seemed very subdued. I put it down to some personal problem and thought no more about it. After all, we cannot always be the belle of the ball, and life carries on and throws up problems out of the ring. I felt that he was just having some quiet time.

The bell announcing the start of the fight rang out loud and clear and I took those few steps to the centre of the ring. He however, stayed in his corner. This was unusual, I thought, and I proceeded to go towards him. As I started to move, he quickly crouched down and with a pitiful cry and put his arms over his head. Bloody hell I thought, what's going on here then?

There were several mumblings from the crowd, which eventually developed into slow hand-clapping. The referee, who thankfully had several years' experience under his belt, sent me back to my corner and knelt down in front of the other wrestler and quietly spoke to him. This whispered conversation went on between them for about a minute. Then the wrestler was gently taken back to the changing room.

Finally, the Master of Ceremonies was brought back into the ring and announced that due to events beyond our control, this bout would not take place. Another wrestler was brought into the ring and my fight began. It wasn't the best fight I'd ever had, mainly because of my concern for my first opponent. We did however continue and provide the audience with the sort of entertainment that they had paid for and indeed, deserved.

When I finally made it back to the changing room, I was to hear something that had never even crossed my mind. Apparently, it was a case of 'ring fright'. I had never heard of this before. For some reason better known to a psychiatrist, it is a form of stage fright where suddenly, and for no apparent reason, the unlucky bloke is frightened of wrestling, and his mind can no longer focus on what he was supposed to do. He finds himself shying away from a situation which a few days ago he would have taken in his stride.

"But this can't be happening!" I remonstrated. "He is one of the best."

"Ye better believe it laddie, it could be any one of us" said old Jock, a Scottish wrestler, shaking his head in a pitying sort of way. "It's no the first time and it will no be the last."

"Well, can he be cured?" I asked.

"Who knows?" said another bloke. "In a lot of cases they get over it but he'll never fight again, that's for sure."

"Why not?" said another.

"Because no promoter will take the chance, you don't get a second go with this problem."

"Callous bastards!" I shouted.

"Not at all" said another. "That's life. If you suddenly had epilepsy, they would take your driving licence away from you, it would be nothing personal but for the safety of others, it is the right thing to do."

The more I thought about it, the more I came to accept that what they were saying was right, even if I did think it was a bit harsh. What would I do if I could never wrestle again? It didn't bear thinking about.

It took me several months before I could put this event to the back of my mind and even begin to come to terms with it. Like many other wrestlers, I took it upon myself to visit him at his home whenever we were travelling that way. Both he and his wife would always make us welcome with a cup of tea and a slice or two of homemade cake. She would then leave us to have a catch up on what was happening in the world of wrestling and to mull over old times.

It was many years later when I heard that the well-known darts player Eric Bristow would suffer a similar fate and find he physically could not let go of the dart. Life can seem so unfair sometimes.

Storm in a teacup

As you can imagine, it is just not possible to go through a whole career in wrestling without sometimes finding yourself in confrontation with an avid and highly excited fan, or a drunkard in the bar afterwards. I, like many others, have my own way of dealing with this enforced situation, and that is, wherever possible, buy them a drink. It usually works, unless the perpetrator is unreasonably drunk and, then he will be dealt with by the bar staff long before it gets to that stage.

I had been used to dealing with the drunken element in my days on the fairgrounds. You don't need violence - just turn them round quickly a couple of times, then stand back and let nature take its course. They usually have other things to deal with and the bar staff have to clean up the mess.

Without a doubt, the most difficult situation to deal with is caused by staying over at the place where you have performed the night before and going out to shop the next day. Someone from the audience is bound to be shopping at the same time and accost you in the High Street. Usually it's a group of elderly ladies who were incensed at my antics in the ring the night before, and would never give up a chance to, at the very least, reprimand you. More often they will give a load of verbal, much to the amusement of the passers-by, who no doubt think I must be a nasty piece of work to upset these dear old souls. You would have thought I had mugged them for their pensions. Of course, retaliation was, and quite rightly so, out of the question, and to offer any form of explanation or apology useless. If they were members of the local WI then look out, you were doomed from the start.

I am sure that the members of the WI were nice people and I would be the first to applaud that great institution, but they appear to be the nearest thing this country has to the Mafia. Perhaps I am being unkind, but then I speak as one who has, more than once, agreed to speak to their groups on the joys of wrestling. It was not unheard of for me to get a good hand bagging, or a dig in the leg from an umbrella.

The one I remember most vividly happened while I was wrestling in Halifax. It was a Monday night and I had the following day to myself before fighting in Leeds on the Wednesday. I decided that I would spend Sunday looking at the wonderful places in that area and travel to Leeds early afternoon on the Wednesday. I was enjoying a leisurely coffee and reading a newspaper in a café somewhere in the shopping area of Halifax when an elderly man and his wife came in and sat at the table across from me.

"I know you!" she shouted at the top of her voice, "You dirty sod." Everyone in the café turned round and stared at me. I did the only thing I could and hid behind my newspaper. "It's no good hiding," she continued. By this time, I had the feeling that everyone in the café thought I was some sort of a pervert. The owner came over to see what the commotion was, and my word, she was going to tell him, as well as anyone else in the vicinity who could hear her. She was remonstrating with the owner about how disgusting it was that he should allow someone like me into his establishment and that she was going to make sure it was reported to the authorities. I was getting quite concerned at this point, not for myself, but that she would soon have a heart attack, if she carried on.

I left my payment on the table and was just about to leave when the owner stopped me. "Oh no, you didn't start it, if anyone should leave it should be her" he said.

"Look, I don't want any fuss and I have finished my coffee," I said, but he wasn't having any of it. Right was right, and she should leave. By this time, the rest of the café had heard everything and realised that I was not actually a pervert and had only been doing my job. The whole episode was getting quite out of control. Then the husband of the lady, who had up until that point been silent, suddenly burst out laughing. I looked around to see the old lady doing the same, and indeed, the owner. I was bemused, as was the rest of the café.

It turned out that the lady was the sister of the owner and, with her husband, she had concocted the whole episode when they saw me, as they had indeed been at the wrestling on the Monday and were all fans of the game. The owner relayed all this to the bemused customers and I received a round of applause. I stood up and nodded in appreciation (I wanted to kill him really), then settled down to another cup of coffee, on the house. After signing a few autographs, mainly on the backs of serviettes, I politely posed for a photograph with the owner and staff, and after declining an invitation to lunch, I took my leave.

At least I had managed to make someone's day, even if the whole thing had totally embarrassed me. All I wanted was a quiet cup of coffee and a read of the paper.

I name this rose

One early spring day towards the latter end of the seventies I found myself on my way to Norfolk for an evening of wrestling with a difference. It was the trend at that time for the rose growers of the country to pick out famous people who would have a particular strain of rose named after them. In order to further the publicity, they would choose some obscure venue for the presentation. The venue for this particular evening's wrestling would also be the venue for the naming ceremony. Having never been a part of anything like this before, I didn't know what to expect.

The first thing that hit me when I entered the great hall was the quantity of flowers (mainly roses). My god, I thought, it's Chelsea Flower Show. The changing room smelt of a sweet rose petal scent. As I looked about at all the different flowers on display, I thought that at least it was better than the usual aroma of sweat. Before the usual crowd and some distinguished guests arrived, we were all taken into the great hall to be issued with the running order for the evening and warned by the promoter that on this occasion, the breaking of wind would be confined to the changing rooms and whatever we did, we were to mind our language. A few other dos and do nots, and we were released.

I noticed that at the stage end of the hall was a large, dropdown banner that had all the details of this particular rose, how to grow it and what type of soil it preferred, and next to it was another banner with the name and photograph of the lady who was to receive this honour. I am not going to reveal her name, but as personalities go, she was never up there among my favourites. She used to look down her nose at the likes of us and I bet she was beside herself to learn that this great honour would be bestowed upon her at such an undignified event as the local wrestling hall. Still, what did I care? I was earning a living so it would make no difference to me one way or the other. I, like the rest of the blokes, would keep a low profile, go along with the evening, do our job and draw our wages and that would be that.

The bouts went as well as they should, and were it not for the fact that at the end of each bout, the wrestlers were presented with a rose, it was nothing out of the ordinary. Then came the big presentation from inside the ring (once the ropes had been taken down and suitable steps were in place, turning the ring into a platform). Speeches were cordially given, hands were shaken and photographs taken. The two banners were replaced in the ring as requested by the photographer from the local paper and it gradually (and some might say painfully) came to a close. I thought that was the end of it - until a few weeks later I received in the post from a wrestling mate, the cutting from the local paper.

"Hi Jackie, I thought you might find this amusing"

said the note that came with it. I read it and burst into laughter. It was a good write up with a photograph of the lady in question and in the background, the banner with planting instructions to the left of her. It said that as well as giving a good performance in a bed with others, she could always be relied upon to perform much better up against a wall or fence.

Hitting the big time

The late summer of 1975 was a time I shall always remember. It held for me a whole bag of mixed emotions, a real roller coaster of a ride.

It started with a telephone call from none other than the great Joe D'Orazio. As anyone who knew wrestling back in those days will remember, Joe was not only one of the top referees but one of the mainstays of that hallowed institution Dale Martin Promotions, which was part of the set-up of Joint Promotions.

"Hi Jackie, "sang out the familiar voice. "We want you to come for a trial with us. There's a show at Cheltenham Town Hall on Saturday 20th of this month. If you can make it, we'll give you a bit of time afterwards. Is that OK?"

Of course it was OK! Wild horses wouldn't keep me away. I could hardly believe my ears, let alone my good fortune. After all those years I was finally going to get my crack at the big time. The 20th was only a week away, but it was surprising what thoughts would go through my head in that short space of time. Was I good enough? What will the trial consist of? Who will I be fighting? Am I the only one? Is it all just some gigantic hoax?

By the time the big day came round, I had worked myself up into a right state. I had confided in only one person, Ken Banks, my mate from the beginning of my time as a wrestler, who had agreed to come with me.

We set off in good time and arrived promptly at the time agreed. I left Ken at the hall entrance and made my way to the dressing room. I knew the way well, as in my younger days, it was where I had stood in order to collect the many autographs of all my heroes. I politely knocked on the door and entered.

"Can I help you?" said this tall and obviously important man.

"Yes, I have come for my trial, I need to meet with Eddie."

"You've got it wrong, sunshine" came the reply. "There's no Eddie here."

"But I got a message from Joe to come here tonight for a trial?"

"Well you'd better ring him, because I don't know what you're talking about" he replied, opening the door for me to leave.

It was a long and lonely walk back through the hall and out to the car. "What happened mate?" said Ken. I quickly relayed to him the conversation, choking back the tears.

The journey home was a long and silent one, with the occasional question from my mate, who was trying to get his head around the situation.

"You don't think someone has set you up?" he asked. That question had crossed my mind a few times during the week. "No, I don't know anyone that would do that" he said, in answer to his own question. He dropped me off and declined my invitation for coffee.

"Are you going to ring them?" he said. " No" I replied. "I've got my pride to think about." My pride had taken enough of a beating already.

I didn't sleep much that night. I ran the whole experience through my mind a dozen times or more and by the morning, I had quite made up my mind that I would give up wrestling for good. I felt I had failed and anyway, and my heart wasn't in it any more. I would just have to do the fights I was contracted to do and that would be that. Wrestling and I would part company.

A few days later, however, things began to change. I received a letter from Joe in response to that fateful evening in Cheltenham. He apologized for the mix-up, saying that the Master of Ceremonies had had to be changed at the last moment and the new one didn't have any knowledge of me. He assured me he would sort it out and be in touch. Well that put paid to any idea of a hoax, as I now had it in writing, but as to whether they would really contact me, I had my reservations. Clearly, they were not as good as I had been led to believe on the administration side and I had, by then, quite convinced myself that I was consigned to the bin.

I was, however to be proved wrong. Within a short while, I was invited to attend another trial, this time at the Colston Hall in Bristol.

I had never been to this hall before and was amazed at the size and grandeur of the place. I did get my trial with Dale Martin and was asked to do a couple of rounds with a wrestler I had seen and admired for many years, a chap named Vic Faulkner. He was the brother of Bert Royal, and between them they had formed a tag team, the Royal Brothers. Any fan worth their salt, would be able to tell you about the Royal Brothers. I did my best and seemed to impress them, but it would be a while before I would know how I did, as it had to be taken up at a higher level and discussed before the decision was made.

A few weeks later, after I had tried, unsuccessfully, to put it to the back of my mind, I received a telephone call summoning me to London to meet with them. I hadn't been there long when I heard the news I had been waiting for since I was about eight years old. I was in!

Joe shook me by the hand, explaining that it would be about a month before I would start, as all bookings were done at least four weeks in advance, and were there any questions I would like to ask. I swallowed hard.

"Well yes, there is one" I said. "I would actually be on the bill wouldn't I, and not just used as a stand by?" I didn't want just to be at their beck and call when it suited them for when another wrestler had to drop out. This was something I had heard of from other wrestlers. He assured me that was not the case, but said it did sometimes happen and I would, from time to time get that request, as did all the others who worked for them. I understood that, and accepted it.

I left them and caught the train back home with a good sense of achievement. I felt that this time, I was on my way.

The first thing I did that evening was to contact my mate Ken and give him the good news. He knew me well enough to admit that he was the tiniest bit jealous, but he congratulated me on my news, adding, "When you're famous, you won't forget our humble beginnings, will you?" He said it tongue in cheek but with a note of concern in his voice. He needn't have worried, my feet have been and always will be firmly on the ground.

True to their word, the work started to come in a month or so later, and one night I found myself in the town hall bar in a location I can't remember. I had arrived in plenty of time and was relaxing with a coffee when a voice I recognized called out to me, "Hey Jackie, one or two sugars?"

I looked up and saw Jackie Pallo standing there. "I owe you a coffee don't I?" he said smiling. You could have knocked me down with a feather. Fancy him remembering our previous conversation from two years before.

We sat and chatted for a while and he gave me the heads-up on life inside the business from his point of view, told me what to watch out for and who to avoid, and a few other tips that he felt might be handy to me. Then he left for the changing room. I have been in the company of that great man on many occasions since that night and although I would never forget it, it was never mentioned again.

Needless to say, I went on to meet loads of my childhood heroes and over a period of time, I wrestled most of them. I particularly remember meeting that most enigmatic wrestler of all time, Les Kellett. He was, of course, not only a legend to me and loads of fans throughout the country, but he was known among us as the 'wrestler's wrestler'. His name came up during many conversations and I can honestly say I never heard a bad word against him. A prince among men, top of the pile - these were just a couple of the comments that would come our way with regard to this all-time great.

Alas, I never got to fight with Les, for no other reason than it never worked out that way. I have however been in his company many times and always found him very easy-going and utterly charming. For those of you who have never seen him, he would take a certain amount of stick from his opponent and appear to be in a daze about the whole thing, staggering about the ring as though he was about to collapse. Then all of a sudden he would get annoyed. He had the habit of grabbing his hair and pulling it forward so it stuck out at the front, which would signify his disgust. Then he would make a complete fool of his opponent by slightly stepping to one side of his onslaught and sending him off-balance and falling to the canvas. Many a forearm smash would be delivered perfectly by an opponent only to have it land in fresh air, with the result that he overbalanced and ended up in a heap at the referee's feet. He was an opponent's nightmare in the ring, but a thoroughly great bloke this side of the ropes. I heard it said many times that if he hadn't become a wrestler, Les, in his younger days, would have made a fantastic ballet dancer.

There were many good wrestlers about at that time. Some I will mention later and others, perhaps, in another volume. Another good wrestler as well as a thoroughly nice bloke was a wrestler by the name of Pat Roach. Many fans of the early days will remember him in the ring, but I guess most people will know him better as Bomber, one of the seven main characters from that wonderful television serial *Auf Wiedersehen Pet* (more of that later). Pat was a versatile fighter who would be fairly matched against any opponent he fought with. He was an extremely unselfish man and would take great pains with any up-and-coming wrestler to help, advise and generally encourage them. He well deserved the unofficial title of the 'Gentle Giant'.

There were a few differences between my past wrestling ventures and my new ones. I had more work, but I also had further to travel. I don't need to tell you the difference between travelling from Gloucester to Bristol, for example, and from Glasgow to Taunton, as I did in my new life. We did, of course, do the majority of travelling overnight, wherever possible. It was not unusual in one week to go from Scotland to Cornwall, then Newcastle, on to Swansea, then to Manchester, before ending up in Cardiff. You have to remember that in the mid-seventies we didn't have the fast cars or indeed the motorways we have now. In fact it was often so chaotic that digs couldn't be pre-booked because you never knew exactly where you would be at any one time, and those you did manage to book would have to be warned that you would be arriving in the early hours and would need to sleep for most of the day. This was opposite to their usual set-up as they usually wanted you out before 10 am so they could clean up and change the sheets for the next guest. I guess it was OK if you were staying for a week, but one night was different and there were only a few that would allow your nocturnal existence to interfere with their routine.

Many people would mistakenly think that being at the "top of the tree" we would stay in lovely hotels instead of bed and breakfast establishments. Not so. We were jobbing wrestlers, not pop stars. You were lucky if you had a television in the building, never mind being in a position to throw one out of the window.

I remember that the vehicle in which I did most of my travelling was a Ford Granada. Not a bad choice in those days as it had a column gear change, which left one wide seat in the front. Handy for sleeping on in an emergency, when digs were all taken or, as often happened, you ran short of petrol before the garage opened.

As I recall, the motorways were the only all-night petrol stations in those days, and at most stations you were still served by a member of the garage staff. There were no self-service stations in the seventies, though of course the petrol was a fraction of the price it is now - and you got Green Shield Stamps.

Back then I could find my way to most city and town halls in most parts of the country. Ask me about Woolworths or Timothy Whites and I didn't have a clue, but when it came to city halls, I was your man.

With one exception, and that was Cardiff. Lovely as it was, it was a devil to find. Every road I took seemed to end up in Barry Island. In fact I very soon discovered that the best plan was to head for Barry and sort your directions out from there.

The Birmingham area was another headache. It was relatively simple to get there, but the signs that took you in were not so obliging on the way out. I know it is much better nowadays, but back then it was a nightmare.

One question I have often been asked in my later years is whether it was a glamorous life. In fact it was hard work, and believe it or not, the wrestling was the easy part - it was the travelling that took its toll. Don't get me wrong, I was very appreciative of the whole thing, after all, it was what I had worked towards for many years and I was going to get everything out of it I could. There were loads of fantastic opportunities that opened up for me, and I will share some of them with you now.

We are sailing

During a trip to Chichester, we were invited out for a day to sample the delights of the local sailing club. A few of us had been invited by the Committee, several of whom had seen us in the ring on the Saturday night. It was one of those rare times when we had a Sunday off, and our next booking was in Brighton on the Monday. There were three of us present who had been booked on both venues, while the others were setting out for their next booking, or using the Sunday to travel home.

We didn't know what to expect, thinking that these yachting types would talk down to us, as we clearly were not of their standing in life. We were totally on the wrong track and found them to be delightful and welcoming. We got off on the right foot very early on when the captain of the club said, "We don't have to put to sea or anything hazardous like that. If you want to, we can all get pissed in the clubhouse". But it was the general view among us landlubbers that we should at least give this sailing lark a go. After all, we were guests and we didn't want to offend our hosts.

It was a sunny day with a brisk wind as we found ourselves skimming along the water, all wearing life jackets of course - they were safety conscious, even in those days. Health and Safety hadn't been invented then, but we relied upon old-fashioned common sense. Riding on a yacht proved to be easy enough provided that you remembered to look out for the boom, as it swung right across the boat and would knock you into the water without warning.

We had a good three hours on the water. I thought we had travelled at least halfway to France by then, but they said we hadn't even left the harbour. We finally arrived back on dry land, and after a quick wash and brush-up, we sat down to a great meal, topped off with a few beers, and spent the rest of the time relaxing and swapping stories with our hosts.

It was about ten o'clock when we arrived back at our digs, and I was thoroughly exhausted. My two mates went off to sample a bit more of what Chichester had to offer, but I declined and went to bed. I think the sea air (OK, harbour air) had taken its toll. It had turned out to be a fantastic day and our hosts had really looked after us well. The next time I visited that lovely town I was able to reciprocate by taking a few of them out for a curry.

Have you got a light, boy?

One of the best aspects of being a wrestler was being able to visit some lovely places. If you have the right attitude, you can go anywhere and find something interesting to see. Bolton was no exception. Many people who spend their lives in one place would think of Bolton as a very industrial place, full of high, smoke-belching chimneys, grime-ridden streets and men wandering around wearing cloth caps. This couldn't be further from the truth. I found it to be a lovely place to visit. Yes, of course, it's busy, but it is a city, after all. There is plenty for the tourist to see, and like a lot of these places, ten minutes in the car and you can be in the countryside.

As for the City Hall, well, it is what it is, a building of great architecture and history (at least it was when I was there, all those years ago). The people were friendly, the digs were fine and the food was appetizing and plentiful.

This particular night had brought with it one of the most violent thunderstorms I had ever witnessed, and eventually the electricity took a dive. There we were, a hall full of people, my opponent and myself trying our best to entertain them, then - nothing, pitch black. It was not the sort of situation you train for, so what were we to do? We did the only thing we could, and carried on with the bout - or so they thought.

The referee sat in the corner waiting while my opponent and I leaned on the ropes, occasionally stamping our feet and grunting and groaning, but never moving a muscle. The crowd, under the impression that we were still fighting, continued to shout and boo. I believe I received a public warning during this blackout, but what it was for, I will never know.

Eventually, after about ten minutes, the lights came back on. We just continued leaning on the ropes, stamping and grunting as before. The crowd by this time had realised what we had been doing during the period of darkness and started to laugh, culminating in a tremendous round of applause. We restarted the match from the beginning and went on to entertain them as we were paid to do. I think they appreciated the joke and it didn't detract from their evening of enjoyment. The promoter was pleased as well and stated that had we been a military unit, we would have been mentioned in dispatches.

You're my greatest fan

There is nothing guaranteed to entertain you better than a group of pensioners who are out to enjoy themselves. I know it was that age group that was to blame for me getting knocked out in the past, with their handbags and umbrellas and suchlike, but I guess I had to share the blame for that, as I was the one who had got them annoyed in the first place, and anyway, I'm sure that they're not all thugs.

As a rule, once you had finished your fight, it was normal to shower and change and then to go out and watch the rest of the fights, if you were on first or second bout, grabbing yourself a drink on the way (in my case, usually a cup of tea). This particular night in Newcastle, I was, approached by such a group who were after autographs and wanted a chance to tell you what they thought of you, which in my case was usually abusive. This particular night they were a happy bunch, apparently celebrating a birthday. Doris had reached the grand age of 72, and had decided that an evening of wrestling was the way to spend her birthday, so she had come with seven of her friends. They were not in the frame of mind to settle for an autograph and a quick peck on the cheek was demanded, which I cordially supplied.

Photographs were taken, and then the fun started. One of them wanted to take me home and feed me, as apparently I looked a bit undernourished. Another thought I was Freddie Starr in my spare time and a third one wanted to know where I was staying.

"I have to sleep under the ring on a bit of old carpet" I said.

"Oh that's a shame'" said one.

"He's pulling your leg, Beattie," said another, which culminated in me getting a slap on the arm, while she said "You bugger!"

All of a sudden the quietest of the bunch was pushed forward towards me to ask, "Can I have your autograph mister? You are my greatest fan."

"Am I?" I replied, "In that case, I'd better have your autograph as well." She realised what she had said. "You know what I meant" (another slap on the arm). "You can't tell me anything I don't know about wrestling, I've been watching it for years."

"Oh I bet I can, for instance, did you know that it's not just water we drink in the corner, between rounds, they put a load of gin in the bottle, it numbs the pain."

"Does it?" came the reply, then thinking about it, "Aw, you're having me on again!" (yet another slap), and so it went on.

It doesn't do any harm to have a laugh with the crowd - it costs nothing, and in a lot of cases it cheers them up. A good laugh with the right people cheers anyone up and those pensioners certainly were the right people.

Encounter with iron man

This story could be a bit vague in the telling as I might have the wrong person in the wrong place at the wrong time, but I think it is still worth a mention.

The gentleman concerned was a well-known and respected wrestler by the name of Sid Cooper, I think (sorry Sid if it wasn't you), and I believe it took place in Nottingham. I do remember that my friend Pat Roach was there at the time. We had finished our bout and were standing at the back of the hall when Sid entered the arena. It was a thing of his to pick on certain members of the audience on his way to the ring and get them to punch him on the jaw. He, of course, rode the punch in a way that made his jaw seem really tough. It was a trick he had learned as a boy boxer and it came in handy as a bit of showmanship for his audiences.

Unfortunately for Sid, on this particular occasion he had picked on the wrong man. The man in question politely refused, but Sid was having none of it, so the man relented, pulled back his arm and landed his fist on Sid's chin. All through this action, I was trying desperately to attract Sid's attention with a shake of the head, done discreetly of course. Although Sid looked in my direction a few times, he obviously couldn't see me trying to stop him. I knew this particular member of the audience, so I knew what was coming.

Sid was in trouble. The gentleman he had picked on had been in the army and had lost his arm on the beaches of Normandy at the D-Day landings. He had been fitted with a metal arm, and Sid had just been hit in the face with the equivalent of a shovel.

Sid was out for the count. Pat and I rushed forward, as did the first aid people. An ambulance was called and Sid was taken away to the nearest casualty unit and a replacement wrestler had to be brought in from the next nearest available place, which happened to be Sheffield.

The last bout had to be brought forward to give the replacement time to get there. Having fought in the first bout in Sheffield, he then had to rush over to Nottingham and fight in the last bout there.

I never did find out what happened to Sid or what injuries he ended up with, but it was the talk of the hall that night. He disappeared from wrestling for quite a while after that but eventually returned, no worse for his escapade. However I don't believe I ever saw him try to ride another punch from the audience after that.

More than she bargained for

This story is one of those that pop in and out of my memory from time to time, since Pat Roach reminded me of it a few years ago, and it still makes me smile. To save embarrassment I won't mention the venue, but it was one of the smaller ones of the day. We were always made to feel welcome there and we always managed to secure good digs.

On this occasion I was approached by a very nice middle-aged lady who introduced herself as Mollie. We were all used to having a bit of banter with the audiences during and after the show, but Mollie was something different. She had, shall we say, designs on me and my body and pulled no punches in telling me so, closely followed by a graphic description as to what was expected of me if I would care to go to her place afterwards. If I had been of a more sensitive nature I swear I would have blushed. I declined the offer, thanked her very much but informed her that I was busy after the show. "Well if you change your mind, here's my address" she said, handing me a piece of paper.

I was so amused by Mollie that I shared my conversation with another wrestler, a chap by the name of Johnny Yeardsley. "Oh god, not you as well" he said. "That makes six of us. You know what she's done, She's asked us all in turn, until one of us said yes."

At the end of the show, Johnny called a few of us together. "Right, here's what we do lads, we all go round there and knock on the door, one at a time. If we all turn up, then at least we're safe from her clutches. Let's see what she does."

The show finished, as usual, about 10.15 pm and by 11 o'clock we were all on our way to an address just outside the town. We thought we were heading for the seedier side, so imagine our surprise when we pulled up opposite a lovely, spacious detached house in an opulent area.

"Hello" said Johnny, " what have we here?" That's Tom's car over there."

We all burst out in fits of laughter. Tom (I've changed the name of course) was the referee. He had obviously been approached by Mollie and had taken her up on her offer.

Johnny went in first, I followed a couple of minutes

later and so on until we were all in there. Poor Mollie, all she could do was make us cups of tea. Never have I seen a woman so embarrassed. As she served the tea wearing a dressing gown, one of the lads piped up "I owe you an apology my dear, I didn't realise you were inviting all of us. Oh look, you're wearing stockings under your dressing gown, but I thought that you had trousers on at the hall. Do you always wear knee-length leopard skin boots around the house? I prefer slippers myself. What about you Jackie?"

"Oh I'm a slipper man myself," I said. "Did you notice, there's a car outside that looks exactly like Tom's?"

So it went on for a good fifteen minutes, all of us taking turns to put our foot in it, in all innocence (or so she thought). "I'll go and make some more tea," said a rather pink-faced Molly, and quickly left the room.

"OK Tom!" shouted Johnny, "You can come down now, we won't tell anyone." We all took turns to shout up the stairs, "Put your clothes on Tom and come and have a cup of tea, have you been a naughty boy Tom?"

These jibes kept coming for a few minutes until we heard a small voice from upstairs say, "I can't. I'm tied to the bloody bed."

Everyone erupted in laughter and rushed upstairs to witness this spectacle. The sight of poor old Tom was more than we could cope with and several of us collapsed in a heap with laughter. "Who's been a naughty boy then?" said one bloke, emphasizing each word with a loud slap on Tom's bare buttocks.

We finally got back downstairs to find our red-faced host, who by this time was beginning to realise that it was a set up. She had resigned herself to the situation and was laughing with us, mainly out of embarrassment.

Tom came down rather gingerly, fully clothed, and seemed annoyed at Mollie for setting him up. We soon put him right on that score, adding that he only had himself to blame. We stayed for a while and made sure our hostess was none the worse for our visit and assured her that this would go no further, a gesture that was not afforded to Tom of course, who was the laughing stock among the lads for months afterwards.

We also had a whip round and sent Mollie a big bunch of flowers with the words, "thank you for the tea" written on the card. However, nothing was ever again seen of Mollie at the wrestling matches.

Cuckoo in the nest

I have given the title to this story a lot of thought. A cuckoo is a bird that lays eggs in another bird's nest and is quite fitting on this occasion. All will become clear as you read on.

I was wrestling in a London venue when one of the best-known wrestlers at that time cornered me. "Jackie" he said, "are you working next Wednesday night?" I reported that I wasn't. "Great, come and work for me for that night then, I will pick you up at your house, I'll be passing on our way down to Devon."

"OK, but who's the promoter?" I asked.

"I told you, you'll be working for me."

Very mysterious indeed, I thought. Normally, I wouldn't have gone, but this particular gentleman was not only a first class wrestler but a thoroughly nice bloke and one hundred percent genuine in everything he did. I would always be willing to help anyone out with those credentials. I have purposely not mentioned his name, as I am not sure if his contract allowed him to do what we were about to do. Sadly, he has since passed away, but I would not wish any ill feeling to his family and tell tales out of school. For the purpose of this narrative, I will call him Mr Cuckoo.

Mr Cuckoo picked me up as agreed and soon we found ourselves heading for a little town in deepest Devon. I thanked him for inviting me along and told him I felt quite honoured. "You needn't" he said, "I asked four others first but they were all busy. Don't worry, you will be adequately paid for your trouble."

I chuckled and asked what we were doing it all for. He explained that he had heard from a relative who lived in that part of Devon that his name was appearing top of the bill at a small venue, yet he knew nothing about it. I knew enough to know that if he was top of the bill on any poster there was going to be some serious money paid out by the avid fans and it sounded as though someone was out to make a fast buck.

"It's one of the oldest tricks in the book," he said. Apparently, what these unscrupulous promoters do is put a top name on the bill so that they can fill the hall to capacity with wrestling fans paying inflated prices for the tickets. At the last moment, it will be announced that, due to illness or injury, the top name cannot make it but they have, at the last minute persuaded some other wrestlers to stand in. The fans are disappointed, but have to settle for it.

"So what are we going to do then, shouldn't you tell the police? After all, it's fraud" I said.

"We're going to fight. We don't want to disappoint all those wrestling fans, do we? I've got a feeling that the wrestlers on that bill are either beginners or just enthusiastic, but I bet you that there is very little experience on that bill tonight, and they're getting paid peanuts. That's why I asked you to come along. I like to know that my opponent isn't going to do something stupid and cause me unnecessary injury and put me out of work for the next few weeks."

I had got to know Mr Cuckoo over the last few years and soon realised that if someone was stupid enough to, let us say, "take his name in vain", then he would personally see to it that the perpetrator would be brought to book.

We found the place, after a lot of trouble, and before

entering, we took a look at the poster outside. Apart from the name of my colleague emblazoned all over it, we recognized no other wrestler on the bill that night. He squared his shoulders. "Right, now to find Mr Big."

Mr Big turned out to be a weasley little spiv who could have easily been knocked down with a feather when we confronted him in a back room of the hall.

"Oh it was an error at the printers." He said, squirming all over the place. "Error my arse!" said Mr Cuckoo. "Now there are two things we can do here. We can either call the police and have you arrested for fraud, or we can play it my way. The choice is yours." Of course, he had no choice but to roll over.

"First thing, we only work for promoters who pay us in advance. Call us superstitious if you like but we get paid two hundred pounds each. We'll take it now, in cash."

I was shocked, but not as shocked as Mr Weasel. "I know it might sound over inflated, but, looking at the price of tickets here tonight, there seems to be plenty of cash about," said my buddy. The promoter counted out the cash, whimpering and whining. "Thank you" said Mr Cuckoo. "Now I take it that we are top of the bill and on last, so if you don't mind, Jackie and I will just take advantage of the bar facilities. We will of course take up your generous hospitality and put it on your tab."

We retired to the bar area and chatted to a few fans, who couldn't believe their luck that such a well-known wrestling celebrity was gracing their town hall. We stayed for a while and then went to the changing rooms, where we were greeted by the other wrestlers, who also could not believe they would be on the same bill as this great man. The promoter might have tried to pull a fast one, but we managed to make a lot of people happy.

The wrestling went as we thought it would and the first three bouts were not up to much, but what these boys lacked in content, they more than made up for in enthusiasm. We spent a while talking wrestling talk to the other wrestlers as they sat around and hung on to our every word.

Eventually it was our turn to entertain the overcharged audience and believe me, we must have put a great deal more into it than usual because they thoroughly enjoyed every minute of it. However, my friend had not yet finished with the dodgy promoter. When the bout was over, he took over the microphone and made the following announcement.

"Ladies and gentlemen, it has been a pleasure for us to perform here in the ring for you tonight. It is easy to think that all wrestling takes place in the larger cities and on television, but it is evenings like this, in the smaller places, that are the backbone of British wrestling today. I thank each and every one of you for supporting us here and in every venue, all over the country.

"I notice that there are two gentlemen from the Red Cross at the back of the hall, on duty, as ever, so I would like them to come up into the ring along with the promoter." Up they came. "Now your promoter tonight has asked me to present you with a cheque for two hundred pounds, which he is about to make out to the Red Cross Society. How about that for an act of generosity ladies and gentlemen? Give him a big round of applause."

The journey home was a good one. We had taken a potentially criminal situation and turned it round to the benefit of others, including us. It was to be one of the best paydays of my whole wrestling career.

"Thanks" my mate said, as he dropped me off and accepted some petrol money from me. "It would have been easy to have just informed the police, but the people who had paid out their hard-earned cash would have lost out and anyway, he needed teaching a lesson."

He was right of course. I bet it was many a day before he tried a stunt like that again. I like to think he learned his lesson, but knowing that sort, I doubt it.

Just sign on the bottom

One aspect of the wrestling game is signing autographs. Some wrestlers don't like it, but I always remember it's thanks to the fans that we are able to make a living. It costs nothing to give an autograph and exchange a few friendly words. After all, we are supposed to be representatives of the game.

However, I remember one signing session that took

a turn for the worse (or better, depending how you look at it). The wrestling had finished at the venue in Darlington, a venue I had the pleasure of knowing well. I had fought in this great hall on several occasions and always got on well with the local inhabitants.

On this evening, I was taking a few minutes to relax in the company of other wrestlers on a long plush bench outside the changing rooms. As usual, there were quite a few people looking for autographs and this included a party of youngish females who were out celebrating the forthcoming marriage of one of their party. I guess it was a hen party, although I don't remember them being called that in those days. However, there were about fifteen of them who were obviously out for a good time. Amid the autograph signing, a youngish girl came up to me and asked for an autograph.

"I don't have a book" she said, "but I wonder if you would mind writing it on these." She proceeded to rummage in her handbag and pull out a rather large pair of ladies' knickers. Judging by the signatures already in place, I guess I was not the first to be asked. She explained that she kept them pinned to her bedroom wall. I obliged of course, much to the amusement of the others, and in no time her mates had decided it was a good idea too, so up went the dresses and down came the underwear. One wrestler wanted nothing to do with this, but the rest of us gave it our support and signed away.

We thought that would be the end of it, but no. The next minute we were being asked to sign bare stomachs, breasts and backsides. I was busy signing the bare buttock of a young female, noticing that my signature was the seventh one there, and I mentioned to her that as we were using a permanent marker, it would be a while before they would wear off.

"Oh I never thought of that," she said. I added that she would have to refrain from showing her bum to anyone for the next few days. "That's going to be difficult" she said, "I'm the one getting married the day after tomorrow."

I have often wondered what her new husband thought on his honeymoon night. I wondered if they are still married today. Somehow, I doubt it.

Call me tiger

It's not easy to make really good mates in the wrestling game. Some wrestlers you see once a month and others only a couple of times a year. It depends on how the dice falls when the promoters are making up the matches. Consequently, there were well-known wrestlers I never had the opportunity to meet in the whole of my twelve years. This aside, I did manage to become friends with a few. I will use their real names and not their wrestling names in this narrative so as not to cause any embarrassment, as most of them were household names at the time.

We were approached via a promoter to contribute to an article about the world of wrestling by a well-known newspaper. Six of us had been invited to take part and with the permission of the promoter, we were whisked off to a very posh hotel in London. As well as me there was Tommy, Jim, Sammy, Bernie and Layla. Layla was asked to give her angle on women in the ring, as she had been in the game for a few years and knew her way around.

We duly arrived in dribs and drabs and were all present by about seven o' clock in the evening, when we were treated to a slap-up meal, all paid for by the newspaper. Then, along with the reporter and his photographer, we began the interviews. It was about 9.15 when this came to an end and with the pleasantries out of the way, the newspaper reporters took their leave. We had a quick drink at the bar and discussed what we would do for the rest of the evening.

"I mean it's not going to get too frantic here is it?" said Tommy. "I vote we go and look for a bit of action. Who's up for that then?" We all agreed. Well, all except Bernie. Let me tell you about Bernie.

He was probably the youngest of us there. A smashing lad, liked a laugh with the boys despite being mothered to death by his own parents. (Every time he did something a little bit rash, like having a cappuccino instead of a cup of tea, he would ring his mother for permission.) Added to this, he was most painfully shy when it came to the female gender. A girl only had to smile at him and his face would go down to his chest with an embarrassed grin and he would take on a bright pink colour, which would last a good ten minutes. I could not understand this, because when he was in the ring, he would come up with some of the best wrestling you could wish to see, and so quick was he that I would have thought myself fortunate if I had a quarter of his ring talent. Nevertheless, he was painfully shy.

Reluctantly, Bernie tagged along as we hit the hot spots surrounding our hotel that night. "My round" said Sammy as we approached our fourth bar of the evening. "Pints all round is it?"

"Oh I'll have a lemonade" piped up Bernie. Sammy turned around and faced him. "You bloody won't, not when I'm in the chair. You'll have a pint and like it, what are you, man or mouse?"

Cajoled by the rest of us, he reluctantly agreed. "Here you go Bernie, we'll tell your mum in the morning." And Sammy handed round the beers.

It must have been after midnight when we made our way back to the hotel. We would have got there quicker if we hadn't have had to take it in turns to help Bernie, who by this time was legless and singing his heart out at the top of his voice.

"Look" I said as we arrived in the foyer, "Let's get Bernie to his room and get him to bed before he throws up everywhere, then we can have a nightcap at the bar before we all turn in."

Ten minutes later we were in the bar supping tea and working our way through a plate of sandwiches kindly provided by the night staff. The conversation was lively and very soon came around to poor old Bernie. "He's going to have a thick head in the morning" I said, as we all had a giggle at his expense. "Hey, I've got a great idea" said Layla. She leapt up out of her seat. "I'll be back in a minute."

She disappeared, returning a few minutes later with a mischievous look on her face. "Let's hear it then, what have you done?" I asked. When she finally stopped laughing, she informed us that she had gone to her room and taken into Bernie's room a pair of stockings, a suspender belt and a pair of panties and laid them over the headboard of his bed. "We'll rag him in the morning at breakfast. It will either kill or cure him." And with that we all retired for the night.

The following morning saw us sat at the breakfast table awaiting developments. We waited for Bernie. "I knocked his door on the way down" said Jim. "He didn't sound too healthy."

It was a good ten minutes before Bernie took his seat at the table. He never uttered a word, just sat there with his head on his chest, that silly grin and bright pink face. We said nothing for a few minutes and then Layla spoke out. "Oh Bernie, before you check out, can I get my underwear back, I must have left it in your room last night.

"Oh yeah, what's this then Bernie?" we enquired, as if it was the first we had heard of it. Layla then got up and walked to his side of the table, licked his earlobe and said in a stage whisper so we could all hear, "You were fantastic last night, oh, and by the way, do you still want me to call you Tiger?"

The whole table erupted in laughter. Poor old Bernie - I thought he was going to burst into flames. He was the topic of conversation for the rest of the meal. He had no option but to sit there and take the ribbing of a lifetime. We did however tell him the truth at the end, as we all made our farewells and went our different ways. He just raised his head from his chest, looked at each one of us and in a low voice, uttered the word, 'bastards'. His smile and handshake told us that there were no hard feelings; after all, we were all mates.

We saw Bernie many times after that night, and for years after, we would call him Tiger. He never took offence but would just lower his head, give us a silly grin and turn pink. I'm sure he saw the funny side and remembers it well, but somehow, I doubt that he told his mum.

The hangover

I'm not sure whether I want to remember this story, but I can't seem to forget it, so here we go.

I had travelled to Fishguard on the train as I was

temporarily without a vehicle for a few days, but still had to get to the booking. Not the easiest place to reach by train, especially as I was starting from Deal in Kent. Having had to make a few changes at different stations, I arrived later than I had wished. So after ringing around for a taxi, I was forced to drive directly to the venue, and the small matter of digs would have to wait until the show was finished.

I had been fighting in the first half of the show so I decided to leave early and get a good night's sleep before travelling down to Plymouth for my next show. I was just drinking a quick coffee at the bar when I heard a familiar voice from behind me say, "Mr Evans no less". I turned to see a couple of chaps smiling at me. It was Eric and Ned, a couple of old mates from my fairground days. They were staying close by and had decided to give the wrestling a look. One thing led to another and as you might expect, one pint led to another, and another, and so on. We left the hall and made for the nearest pub, where we continued drinking cider until closing time, by which time I was a little bit merry. OK, hands up, I was totally off my face.

I didn't register exactly how much I had drunk until I came round at three in the morning, outstretched on a bench at the railway station. Once I was able to open both eyes at the same time and check that I had my luggage with me, I began to try and piece together the missing bits. How had I got here? My two drinking buddies must have arranged it. I didn't know how, but I was there and they were the only ones who knew my plans. It was a good job I had mentioned it the night before.

With difficulty, I managed to sit up and take stock. Had I been drinking, or had I spent the evening being hit in the head with a cricket bat? I tried to clear my head. I coughed to at least clear my throat. Not a good idea, I thought, as I felt both of my eyeballs bounce down and hit the platform before springing back into their sockets, or at least that's what it felt like.

I gradually creaked my neck around from left to right and realised that I was the only one in the station. It looked as if an all-night buffet was out of the question. I smiled to myself, which was another big mistake. I would have to remember that for the next few hours - facial expressions were a total impossibility. I tried to count my blessings - at least it was summer and although I was cold, I hadn't got hypothermia yet, and I would be in time for my train, though when it would arrive and where it would be going to I had no idea. Still, wherever it went, it should be heading for civilization, which was a damn sight better than the place I was in now.

I raised myself to my feet rather gingerly and swayed about for a second or two until I had got used to the altitude of 5ft 4 inches and set off in search of a tap in order to stave off the dehydration that comes as a result of a good skinful.

I wandered slowly around the deserted station, to no avail. Waiting room locked, toilets locked, John Menzies newspaper hut locked. Sod it. I wandered outside into the lane and looked around. I could hardly believe my luck, for in the field opposite stood a horse trough. It would have water in it and if I was very fortunate, a ballcock with fresh running water, so it would be safe to drink. All I had to do was negotiate an iron gate. It was locked of course, but if I was careful I would be able to scale it and drink to my heart's content.

After a five-minute struggle I had reached my goal. As I stooped there drinking the fresh cool water I thought to myself that there must be quite a few people in the nearby town that were safely sleeping in their beds, not knowing that one of the stars of the ring who they had paid money to see a few hours before was now drinking from a horse trough in a field. Such is the price of fame.

Within a few minutes, I was back, sitting on the bench in the railway station wishing I had never met my buddies and vowing never to drink cider ever again.

After nodding off to sleep a few times and waking up with the coldness of the night biting right through me, I heard the sound of a bicycle coming up the lane. I went to the main entrance just in time to see the stationmaster taking his bicycle clips off and parking his bike in the ticket office. "Good morning" I said, rather louder than I had meant to.

"Morning Sir, can I help you?" he replied.

"I need to get to Plymouth," I said. He looked me up and down. "Best wait for a train then." It was just what I needed at that time of the morning, a bloody comedian.

"So is there one then?"

"Nope. Not to Plymouth, you'll have to go to Swindon first and get one from there. Don't worry, it's the next train in."

I sighed. Swindon sounded so refined compared to this place. I glanced at my watch; it was a little after six in the morning.

"What time does it get in?" I asked.

"Twenty past twelve" he replied. I could have cried.

I attempted to make polite conversation with him in the vain hope that he would put the kettle on, but he made it very clear that he was busy; after all, he had a pot plant that needed watering. I managed to keep a conversation going for a few minutes, which was quite a feat as I was the only one talking while he busied himself doing, well nothing really.

Finally he relented. "What are you doing around here this early?" he reluctantly enquired. I told him of my previous night's work. It was then that he seemed to perk up. "Oh my wife went to see that, she never misses one. I don't go myself, as I have to get up early for work. Never miss it on the telly though."

That was it; got him, hook line and sinker. It wasn't

long before he allowed me to sit by his fireside and made me copious amounts of tea. We chatted on throughout the morning and right up until my train was due and other passengers began to arrive. By this time, I was beginning to feel a bit more human again and wished him well as I boarded my train, after signing a photograph of myself for his wife.

I settled down to my journey, soaking up all the comfort that second-class can supply. I slept soundly in a carriage all of my own until we were a few miles outside Swindon. Luckily, I had about 50 minutes to get my connection, which would take me right into Plymouth, which meant that I had plenty of time for a decent meal. I settled onto the train in good time. I had managed about five hours' sleep during the first leg of the journey, so if I could grab another three hours then I should be OK until tonight's digs in Plymouth. By my calculations, I should be there just in time for my fight, as I knew that I was first on after the interval. Yep, three hours sleep would put me back on track. The forces were smiling on me, I thought.

No such luck. What I hadn't bargained for was that it was holiday time and the carriage was full of screaming kids excited at heading for the coast, complete with bucket and spades and sticky jam sandwiches. I sneered at them, hoping that they could see me through the great swirls of smoke put up by Granddad's pipe and Mum's cigarettes.

Eventually we reached the coast and it was good riddance to the family from hell. I opened a window open and normal breathing was resumed. That was until I was again invaded, by what seemed to be half of the Royal Navy on their way back to their ships. They were nattering about how they had spent their leave and how they were sailing in the morning to foreign climes. There goes any spare time I might have had, I thought as I stood behind the whole fleet waiting for a taxi.

I arrived at the hall with about fifteen minutes to spare and had to rush to get ready. It was at this time that the events of the day and previous night decided to catch up with me and give me a good kicking. I felt rough.

Things came to a head when I was about a minute into the second round. My opponent, a young fresh-faced chap from Taunton, picked me up, turned me upside down and body-slammed me into the canvas. That was it, enough is enough I thought as my head began to spin. I just lay there listening to the counting of the ref. "Eight, nine, ten, out." I could have made the count but I thought bugger it, I was more than content just to lie there looking up at the lighting gantry. If the seconds hadn't tried to help me to my feet, I would have been happy just to stay there for a lot longer. The fact that there were about three hundred people watching me didn't seem to matter.

Luckily I had used my head in Swindon station and had telephoned ahead and booked my digs. For the first time in my life, I pulled my clothes on over my wrestling costume, grabbed my things and fell into a nearby taxi to head for my bed for the night. I was so tired that I didn't even notice the looks of the taxi driver or the landlady at this weirdo standing in front of them wearing silver boots and full make-up.

Out of gas

I know that in today's society, there is very little praise heard for our boys in blue. Forty years ago, they deserved and got more respect. Whether it was just that the old school copper seemed to be more in control or that they were not so tied up in red tape, I do not know, but they did seem to have a different outlook on life.

As we were among those people who used the wee small hours to travel from one venue to another in relative ease, it was inevitable that we would get pulled over by the odd policeman who wanted to know what we were doing on the road at that ungodly hour. We didn't mind, it was to be expected and they were only doing their job. Most of them would stop and have a quick natter before sending you on your way. It was the way it was done in those days. It wasn't always a squad car that would want you to pull over, sometimes you would be flagged down with a torch from some local bobby on the beat with his pushbike. We never thought of it as an inconvenience, it was a part of the journey.

However, one night as four of us were making our way from Manchester to Swindon, due to the car owner's oversight, we ran out of petrol some thirty miles from our destination. We had not been stopped long before a police car pulled up and enquired what we were doing hanging about in a small town at that time of the morning. Our driver quickly explained and asked the policeman if there was an all-night garage open anywhere in the town. He didn't know himself but would radio the station to see if anyone there knew.

He came back with the news that there was one garage that had a petrol machine that would take a pound note and then dispense fuel; it was about five miles away. "Great" said our driver, "I've got a can in the back, would you be willing to run me there in your car?"

"Can't do that" said the policeman "I'm on my own and there are supposed to be two of us before we let anyone in the car, you'll have to walk it."

We tried everything we could to persuade him to help us out but to no avail, he was obviously off duty soon and couldn't be bothered. So there was nothing for it, the driver would have to walk the distance and we would have to wait for him.

Off he trotted, can in hand, much to the amusement of the policeman. After a quick check around the car to see that it was all in working order and an even slower rendition of his own wrestling experiences as a member of the audience with which he bored the pants off all of us for about ten minutes, he jumped in his police car and sped away.

About a minute later, our driver returned with the petrol can. "My god, you must have run all the way there and back, you've only been gone 15 minutes." I said.

"I would have been here sooner if that stupid copper had gone earlier."

"How do you mean?" we said.

"I haven't been to a garage," he said. "I waited until he wasn't looking and siphoned some from a few of those cars. They won't miss it, I took a little bit from each one."

We all fell about laughing. "Good job he didn't catch you" I said.

"Too right" said the driver, "most of it came from the police car."

We carried on our way with enough petrol to get us to our destination and a note on the dashboard to remind us to fill up in the morning.

My finest hour

During my career as a wrestler I have been through several phases, from being laughed at to ignored, unheard of, known locally, fairly well known nationwide and finally quite popular. Sitting here now and thinking back, I have to say that my favourite time was the early seventies. It was that time of the birth of glam rock when famous singing stars and groups took to wearing colourful clothes and having long and elaborately-fashioned hair, makeup and glitter - something I had already been doing for several years. I guess my popularity then had little to do with being a talented wrestler and more to do with fashion, but suddenly, and indeed it came as a big surprise to me, I was in fashion. This was a two-edged sword, as in order to capitalize on this good fortune I had to start wearing clothes that were considered to be in the style of the glam rock scene all the time, and not just in the ring. My performances would have to start whenever I was in public and be continuous, right up until I was on my own. That was going to be a tall order for someone who much preferred to wear normal everyday clothes.

That was my lot from that time. A trip to the local shops to buy tight silver jeans and boots with four inch platforms (in silver of course) and a variety of bright (and to my mind, hideous) tops. Wearing those things in the ring was one thing, but did I really have to look such a prat out of it? According to my promoter, it looked great. Easy for him to say, he wasn't the one who was going to have to drive in those boots. I soon fixed that one by wearing a pair of comfy shoes in the car.

I drew the line when he wanted me to buy a matching shoulder bag that looked to me like a handbag, and he realised that to insist would be pushing his luck, so I got away with it. All in all, I spent the next few years walking around feeling a right Jessie.

Looking back on it now, I seemed to remember that it did change a lot of things in my favour. Very soon, I started to notice that some of the younger ones in the crowd took to wearing similar clothes to me whenever I was appearing on the bill. They would wait at the door and cheer as I arrived, and would vie for my autograph and want to be photographed with me. It felt good. I was even mobbed by the crowd on the way in. I would be lying if I didn't say that I loved every minute of it. The promoters also noticed it and I soon found myself being moved up the billing on the posters until finally, I was top of the bill. Every promoter wanted me. I had made it to the top.

Or had I? Sadly, it didn't last. After about three years, as I had expected, I dropped out of fashion and it was back to the same spot on the posters. The promoters stopped paying me high prices and some stopped ringing altogether. Never mind, at least I was still working and at long last, I could get rid of those awful clothes and boots and start wearing my old clobber again. At least I had been given the chance of tasting it, most people don't. I still have the photos to prove that it wasn't just a dream. Oh, and a bunion from those damn boots.

The wrestler's top ten questions

When people want to talk about the world of wrestling (which happens a lot) they invariably ask questions. I will take a while to answer these in the best way I can. The first one is that classic question, "is it fixed?" I have dealt with this one previously in this book. I trust my answer met with your acceptance. Below, I will deal with the next ten questions in order of their popularity.

1. Do you get hurt?

As with all activity in or out of the sporting world, injury is always a factor to be taken into account. I myself have had the odd injury. Landing on the canvas can cause a problem if it doesn't happen properly. We are all taught to land correctly but we don't always get it right, especially if a large opponent lands on top of you. If you remember that some people injure their backs by just picking up a pencil off the floor, it is a wonder that we get away with it all. The answer is yes, we do get injured, but luckily, no more or less than let's say a rugby player. We used to employ several ways of dealing with minor injuries. Wrestlers would often help each other with limb dislocation by popping back the offending joint. It was still sore for a while, but at least you could use it.

The other thing that springs to mind is that most wrestlers (myself included) would carry a needle and cotton, so that if the need arose, we could put our own stiches in, in the event of a deep cut or suchlike. This may sound a bit barbaric but it did save precious travelling time as opposed to sitting in casualty for hours on end. Though what Health and Safety would have made of it in this day and age, I shudder to think. We did suffer from rope burns and the odd mat burn. However, this was not classed as an injury, more as an occupational hazard.

2. What's the money like?

This would depend on your commitment to the game and whether you were willing to travel. Like a lot of things, the work was out there if you were willing to put yourself out and get it. As to the money, that would depend on who you were working for. When I started on the fairground booths, I would get the princely sum of ten bob a fight (50p in today's money). With the independent promoters, you would get £5, which included your travel to and from the venue. The top television people would have got about £25 in those days, which was a good wage if you had enough work available to you. Of course, once you were a household name you would supplement this by opening functions such as leisure centres and the like. The amounts rose over the twelve years I was in the game, but the rise would be matched by the rise in the cost of daily living, and in my case, the cost of any motoring expenses and travelling. What they get in wrestling circles today, I have no idea. One wise wrestler said to me once that if it was just for the money, you wouldn't bother.

3. How do you get on the TV?

Not every wrestler was going to have the chance to fight on television. Some tried but never made it, while others wouldn't have touched it with a barge pole. I myself never thought much about it. Television may have brought the world of wrestling into the living room, but if it was your only means of viewing the game you would be restricted to seeing a mere handful of wrestlers. If however you took yourself around to the different venues available to you, then you would see a greater variety of wrestlers and a lot more skill than you could ever hope to see in your living room.

It was always claimed that to get into television wrestling, you had to be one of the chosen few. In my view, and the view of most if not all of my fellow wrestlers, there were too many rules and restrictions put upon the individual, and from the promoters' angle, it was the right thing to do. The biggest fear among the promoters was that they would lose the franchise that was so dear to them, so they would not take chances unnecessarily. They were permanently walking on eggshells, and knowing how quickly the demise of wrestling came about once the television cameras were finally turned off, I can't say I blame them.

4. What made you want to be a wrestler?

I'm sure every wrestler will have his (or her) own reasons for wanting to wrestle. Firstly, it will depend on what they want out of it and, more importantly, what they are willing to put into it. Like any job, there are those who want to make a career out of it and at the other end of the spectrum there are those who are happy just to make a bit of pin money. For instance, there were always good, experienced wrestlers working the fairground booths when they were set up within reasonable distance. They were happy to go along of an evening and earn a few bob, but were not interested in any travelling. I had wrestling mates who, for various reasons, only wanted a couple of bouts each month. Perhaps they were married and had families to consider, or maybe they worked away. They all had their own reasons. Then there were people like me, who had wanted to wrestle from an early age, and couldn't get enough of it.

For my own part, I soon realised that to be able to wrestle a lot, I would have to try and make a living at it. I guess you could say I fought to live in order to live to fight. It suited my needs, my desires and certainly, for a while back there, I made it my life. In many walks of life, you have to make your own luck and bring about your own opportunities. Of course, skill is a different thing. I knew many skilful fighters who would show up even the best of the television wrestlers, when all they wanted out of the game was the odd few pints of beer.

5. Do you have to be big to wrestle?

Unlike most sports, wrestlers come in all shapes and sizes, although, in my opinion, once a body gets past a certain size and weight, they cease to be wrestlers in the traditional sense of the word and are just men who use their bulk to overpower an opponent. Take the two well-known wrestlers of the eighties, Big Daddy and Giant Haystacks. No one in their right mind would ever have called them skilful exponents in the art of wrestling. They did possess a few of the wrestling moves that were expected of a fighter, but on the whole they were what became known as 'push and shove merchants' (not my own words). That's not to say they weren't entertaining, or indeed popular.

On the other hand, I was good friends with a wrestler in my early days who wrestled under the name of Johnny Diamond. He was about five feet in height and had the build of a hungry whippet. For my money, he was one of the best and most skillful wrestlers that it was ever my pleasure to come across. Even at the height of my career, I would have given my eye teeth to have possessed a quarter of the skill he would display before an audience.

So the answer to the question is - no. In my opinion, there were four types. The first three were small, medium and large. The fourth type were too big to be wrestlers in the traditional sense. They were just good grunt and groan, belly butting, steamrolling entertainers.

6. What is your opinion of women wrestlers?

I feel privileged to state that during my time, I have met and shared the bill with a number of women wrestlers and I must say, in all honesty, that I always found them to be good wrestlers, nice people and a pleasure to know. There were a few I met over the years and I know they won't mind me talking about them. If my memory serves me correctly, there was Klondyke Kate, Mitzi Mueller and Miss Karina, to name but three, as well as many more. OK, they did use colourful language from time to time, but then again, didn't we all? I'm not going to tell you anything seedy about any of them, as there would be nothing to tell. They gave good, all-round entertainment value and were great fighters and more importantly, nice people. I wouldn't hear a bad word about any of them. They all had their part to play in the world of professional wrestling and they did it well.

7. Were you ever scared of an opponent in the ring?

I was never scared of another wrestler, but sometimes I was scared of the unknown. My very first bout was scary in its way because I didn't know if I was capable of putting enough into it to please the crowd. I don't know if scared is the right word, I would say apprehensive is nearer the mark. As a dirty wrestler, I was sometimes afraid of the onslaught of the crowd as they bayed for my blood. In the early days you would get some grief from the occasional wrestler for various reasons. I think they did it to frighten you, as it made them feel superior in some way, although I have never been and never will be intimidated by my fellow man. Some people seem to think that the word 'wrestler' conjures up images of crime, vice and violence. If these things did occur, then I must have been looking the other way. I have had the opposite experience when I have sat next to a 20-stone wrestler in the changing room and listened to how he planned to arrange the flowers at his daughter's wedding. I was present when at the end of a show, a wrestler got down on one knee and proposed to his girlfriend in the ring. Six wrestlers were among those that shed a tear or two, and they may or may not have included me. I never met a wrestler who would scare anyone intentionally and some, including yours truly, would have been mortified if he had thought for one minute that he had done so.

8. What do you think of wrestling today?

To be fair, I haven't seen a lot of it, so my opinion is not based on knowledge, more on first impressions. There seems to be a lot of hype involved, which I believe is an American thing. They seem to spend longer arguing with each other than they spend wrestling. In my humble opinion, it is far removed from the wrestling of my day. The skill of the individual wrestler has given way to the character of the fighter. Perhaps it has to be that way. It is certainly popular and has a worldwide following, bringing about a multi-million pound industry. I own up to the fact that all those years ago, we were thought of in some quarters as showmen and for the enjoyment of the audiences, this was partly true. Yet I like to think that we were competent at our sport. Today's fights seem to be 100 percent showmanship. Nothing wrong with this, it's just that I guess that I'm of the old school.

I do not follow it today but I wish them luck and hope that it affords them a living for many years to come.

9. Have you ever regretted your time as a wrestler?

Not for one minute. If I had my time over again, given the same situation, I would do it all again. Of course, I have made mistakes and some bad decisions, but I am more than satisfied with the results. I have met some interesting people and been in some interesting situations and places. There was a time when I could have navigated my way to most town halls in the country. There was nothing better than being in a hall and experiencing the buzz of excitement and anticipation given off by an enthusiastic band of wrestling fans. It was a pleasure to have been part of it. Even after all these years, I still get to talk to people about wrestling and have the satisfaction of knowing that had I not been a wrestler we might never have spoken to each other. I have wrestling to thank for not becoming a lonely old man.

10. Do you suffer any lasting damage from your wrestling days?

Of course. I need a new pair of hips and I have permanent damage to the blood valves in my left leg. Although I can't be sure this is all because of wrestling, it does seem more than possible. In this world, you don't get anything for nothing - there is always a price to pay.

I sat down a while ago and, with the help of a calculator, worked out that I must have spent 1,800 hours in the ring during my career. That equates to 225 working days or 45 weeks of solid wrestling and being thrown about. Not to mention the travelling I have done, which works out at about 21,600 hours on the road. That's scary. Looking at it, I think I've got away lightly. Looking on the bright side, it probably sharpened my memory, or I wouldn't have been able to write this book.

A wrestler's postbag

Towards the final stage of my career, I got letters from many wrestling fans. Some of them were sent care of other wrestlers, some would filter down from the promoters, but I guess that 80% would be posted or left at the town halls where I was due to wrestle. Some of them were the usual run-of-the-mill stuff, while a few of them were quite saucy in their content. Others were amusing, while a few were heart-rending. I included a few below from right across the board, although there were others that would be considered unprintable. Some of them would make even me blush to read them, and some were not only offensive but physically impossible.

Of course, I have taken out all names and addresses, as they were written to me personally and I do not wish to cause anyone any undue stress or embarrassment. I hope you will read them and take them with a pinch of salt and not be offended or think badly of me, as by today's standards, some of them may not be quite politically correct. They are by no means unique, as many wrestlers were furnished with much the same correspondence during their time in the ring.

Dear Mr Evans

I have been a wrestling fan for the last twenty years and I must say, that the performance that you gave at the ******* Hall last Wednesday was the worst I have ever seen. It was grossly unfair that you should pick on your opponent's left leg to get a submission, just because he had it heavily bandaged. I have always thought that you were made of better stuff than that.

Therefore, when I next see you in action, I have to warn you that I shall not be cheering for you any more until you mend your ways in the ring.

I am sorry to have to tell you this and I know that you will probably be upset at my decision but you have driven me to it.

Yours truly,
****

Dear Mr Evans

I saw you fight last night and thought you were c**p.

From. *********

Dear Jackie,

You don't know me but my husband and I have seen you wrestle many times in the past and I wondered if you would be willing to do me a great favour. My youngest son has informed us that he is gay and this has devastated my husband. He doesn't seem to be able to come to terms with this and I wondered if you could have a word with him as he isn't talking to his son at the moment and it is causing a great deal of tension and heartache in our whole family. He knows you and thinks that you are funny so it might come better from you. I have enclosed my address and telephone number and hope that you are willing to help.

Yours truly
Mrs ********

Dear Jackie Evans,

As I am one of your greatest fans and marvel at some of the costumes that you wear in the ring, I feel that you have a flair for colour and style. Therefore, I would appreciate your opinion on some curtains that I am thinking of making for the lounge. The next time that you are here at the **** Hall, I will bring along the fabric and if you are agreeable to see me, I would value your opinion. I might bring some cushion covers for your opinion as well.

Yours faithfully, *********
P.S. I will introduce myself properly then.

Dear Mr Evans,

I am writing to you because you seemed to be the kindest of all the wrestlers. My best friend and me were wondering how the wrestling ring was made, so when we see you at the wrestling next time, would you let us have a good look at your ring. Love ★★★★★★★ aged 8.

Hey Jackie,

Can you settle an argument between me, and my mate? We are a couple of car mechanics and have this ongoing thing where he says that you're not really a poof and I reckon you are. Next time you are here, can you announce it in the ring before you start?

Hello there Jackie,

My best friend is getting married next month and wondered if you could attend her pre wedding party. I have enclosed an invitation and written the address on the back. She will be surprised to see you there, especially if you wear your wrestling gear and do a slow striptease for her. We are willing to have a collection to pay you if you wanted to book into a hotel for the night.

Yours truly,
★★★★★★★★★★

Oi you big poof,

If, you continue to fight dirty in the ring any more, you might find that you get a punch the next time I see you.

Name withheld.

Dear Sir,

May I say what a wonderful show, you put on for us on Monday evening at the ***** City Hall in *****. My name is ***** and I would very much like to take you out for a drink to a lovely little gay bar that I know. Perhaps, if you are agreeable, you could stay the night. Please contact me on the following number at your convenience.

I remain,

Yours in hope

P.S. I am a single man so there are no complications.

Tall stories and short careers

Over the years I have seen many wrestling personas and gimmicks come to light. Some were good, some less so. Occasionally one would come up that was not so well thought out and ended in a complete disaster. A couple that spring to mind are as follows.

The silver statue

A wrestler who was known to me as Big Ron had decided that he needed a gimmick. He bought himself some silver trunks and boots and on the first night of his creation, covered himself from head to toe in a silver powder purchased from a stage make up specialist. I was on the bill that night but thankfully not fighting him.

It was a fiasco from the start. Everyone in the changing room complained of being dowsed in a fine layer of silver dust as Big Ron powdered himself with the aid of a brush not dissimilar to a shaving brush. He then proceeded to put the dust in his eyes and had to wash it out, leaving a film of dust in the sink, much to everyone's annoyance. Finally, he left the changing room for the ring. I wondered what he was going to do as the Silver Statue. If he was going to stand in the corner motionless, it wasn't going to be much of a show.

It was pretty standard stuff for the first couple of rounds and apart from showering everyone near him in a fine dust, every time he hit the canvas he could quite easily have got away with it. It was in round three that disaster struck. By this time he was beginning to perspire as any wrestler would, and very soon, his powdered covering began to take on the consistency of dough. His opponent, who was finding him very slippery and difficult to hold, succeeded in pulling away vast chunks of what can only be described as silver mud. He wiped his hands on the canvas and tried once more to effect some sort of wrestling hold on his now less-than-silver opponent. The areas of skin exposed from the silver had by now turned a dirty white. For a while it looked as though he was suffering from some deadly skin disease. When this had passed he took on the appearance of a statue that had been at the mercy of every passing pigeon for miles around. The ring looked like a swamp as by this time both wrestlers were slipping and sliding around like a couple of ballerinas. By this time the referee had slid to the canvas a few times and was obviously not in control of the situation, so he decided to abandon the match.

"I don't think I'll pursue that line any more" said big Ron, as he cleaned out the plughole in the shower for the third time. "It didn't go too well did it?" He had to dodge towels, coke cans and other missiles that came his way from his disgruntled workmates. He wasn't too bothered - until he received cleaning and laundry bills from most of the people who had come into contact with him on that fateful night.

Wrestler in shining armour

It seemed like a good idea, but it was doomed from the start. Graham, who was a good enough wrestler without a gimmick, had decided to act out something that he had been thinking about for a few years, and that was to change his name to Sir Camelot and enter the ring in a suit of armour. He would, of course take it off to wrestle. Well that was the theory anyway. As you know, theories have a habit of going belly up at the first possible moment.

It took him a good five minutes to get into his armour, even with the help of a few of us strapping him and buckling him into it. It never occurred to him that he would have to get out of it by himself at the other end. He was duly announced into the ring as usual and apart from all the clanking as he walked and one particular deviation from the aisle and into a concrete pillar en route, he arrived at the ringside.

Now as those of you who have seen a wrestling match will know, the average athletic wrestler would put one foot on a chair, spring himself up onto the ring apron and more often than not, leap over the top rope and into the ring. Not Mr Camelot. He couldn't even get one leg on the chair. No matter how he tried, he couldn't do it, much to the amusement of the crowd.

By this time, the Ref, the Master of Ceremonies, the timekeeper, two seconds and a member of the audience were on hand to give him some much-required assistance. After a lot of pushing and pulling and a lot of head scratching, they decided to lie him on his back against the ring and slide him under the bottom rope. This went well until the breastplate got caught under the rope. When they let go, it shot him back out of the ring like a catapult and right into the front row.

By this time, having viewed the whole episode from the back of the hall, the tears were running down my face, so much so that my make-up was beginning to run. A few minutes later he was in the ring and the aid of the ref and his second got him to his feet and into his corner. Well that was an amusing ten minutes, I thought. But it wasn't over yet. The poor second had to undo about fourteen different buckles and straps, which as you can imagine, took time. All this was accompanied by shouts of "Anyone got a tin opener?" and "How about a sardine key?" No wonder he got flustered.

Amid all the laughter and jeers from the audience, we could detect that the faint murmurs and gurgling from inside the helmet had turned to loud grunts and eventual panic from Mr Camelot, which expressed itself in a swift arm movement, still attached to a metal gauntlet, right across his second's head, producing a nasty head gash. The man was swiftly whisked off by the St Johns Ambulance team to the nearest hospital. Meanwhile with the aid of the referee and one other member of the team, Sir Camelot was free, red as a beetroot and in no fit state to fight anybody.

It was the referee's decision to abandon the match. Probably just as well, as with the amount of time it had taken we wouldn't have been finished until midnight and most of the audience would have missed their last bus home.

I was on next (once I'd fixed my make-up, that is). It was a quiet affair as I remember, nothing much to make it stand out, but then, Mr Camelot was a hard act to follow. Nothing more was heard of him. Graham went back to his usual way of doing things, but would never talk about that night again. I can't say I blame him.

Stage fright

Occasionally, and a good thing too, one of us was called upon to be a stand-in opponent for a new wrestler who was auditioning (for want of a better word) with a promoter. I was always glad to help out as I remembered well those that had done the same for me. This usually entailed having to be at the hall about an hour earlier than normal so that the trial could take place before the crowds started to arrive. I have to say that on the whole, these proved very successful and I like to think I have been instrumental in furthering some wrestling careers.

However, there were a few that were not quite so good and one or two that were a total disaster. I would like to tell you of a couple of these now. Please note that for obvious reasons, I have not used their names, as I do not wish to cause any embarrassment to anyone.

The first that comes to mind was back in the mid-seventies, and I believe it was in the Bristol area. I stood in the ring awaiting my opponent. The only other people present were the referee, the promoter and the new boy's mother and girlfriend. The young wrestler got into the ring. He seemed to be a confident lad as he leaped over the top rope and tested the spring of the ring, before taking to his corner, and having the referee check his boots and hands for sharp objects. As it was a trial, there were none of the usual introductions and so it was off with the jacket and straight in to round one (usually we do three rounds of three minutes duration).

When the bell rang, I took up my position in the centre of the ring and waited for him to do the same. He just stood there and looked at me, looked at the referee and the promoter and without any compunction, proceeded to wee himself. There followed an awkward silence for about 30 seconds, when the promoter cleared his throat and said " well… yes… you don't appear to be ready for the ring yet lad."

The referee and I left the ring and returned to the changing room without exchanging a word. I think we were all shocked at what we had just witnessed. It was totally unexpected, but then nerves were to blame no doubt.

I never came across that young lad again, but I often wondered if he ever got over his nerves and tried at some later stage to enter the world of wrestling.

Another one I remember working with had sailed through his trial and even came up with some moves I had never seen before. I must say he was a pleasure to work with, very skilful and as quick as a mongoose. He's going to do well in this game, I thought. It was a good two months later that I spoke to that particular promoter about him. "How's he doing?" I asked. "Is he getting plenty of work?" The promoter thought for a moment and then replied, "Oh yes. I remember him. Only tried to use him once, he let me down."

"You mean he didn't turn up?" I said in some surprise.

"Oh he turned up all right, but he got into the ring and froze. Turned out that he was scared stiff of all the people watching him. Couldn't even take his jacket off."

You could have knocked me down with a feather. I guess he would have had to call it a day after that. Apart from hypnotherapy, I don't think it's possible to get over that particular type of phobia, and I'm sure that is what it was because with us old dogs, there's nothing we like better than to get up in front of all those people to try to entertain them in the way we have chosen. The majority of wrestlers I have met are good wrestlers but even better show-offs.

Before we proceed further, I would like to make one thing quite clear. By now, some readers may be feeling that I appear to come over as quite an innocent person, that butter wouldn't melt in my mouth, and it was all a jolly jape. Let me make it clear that as a young lad I was no different from the rest. I've had my moments and enjoyed all of the ones I never got caught for. Boys will be boys, as the old saying goes, even more so when you get a bunch of hardened and well-travelled wrestlers together. There are many instances which having reached the age of responsibility and care of others, I would not dream of including in this book. Anyway, I don't think they would print it, and I'm damn sure I wouldn't own up to half of it.

Having said that, the period we are talking about was the late 60s and 70s, and there was always that dividing line that you did not cross. We had something you don't get much nowadays, called respect. Not only for your elders but your fellow man, and most important, for yourself. We never used bad language in front of women and children and most people had standards and stuck to them. It all helped to make life easier in its way. I'm not saying there's anything wrong with the way life is today - it was just different then.

I'm not here to moan about the world or inflict my standards on anyone. I'm just pointing out how it was. Perhaps it was just easier to get away with things then. I guess what I'm saying is that with the passing of the years, you tend to remember the good times and not so much the bad. The world is no different now from the way it always was, it's our memories that change. It seems that the older you get, the less you want out of life and the more critical you become. Well that's my excuse to the younger generation as to why I have become a miserable bugger.

What's the point to all this rambling? Well I will tell you. Many years ago, there was one wrestler I didn't get on with. In fact, thinking back, the repercussions could have been a lot worse. We hated each other from the first time we met. I will not give his name, but he was one of the top television wrestlers and would be known to everyone. He hated anything that related to homosexuality, and though I and several other wrestlers assured him that I wasn't really gay, he was having none of it. He hated me and I hated him for his over-inflated attitude and ego.

It was only a matter of time before we met each other in the ring. There was, as you can imagine, a fair amount of bloodshed. He lost some teeth and I had a broken toe and a crack in my jaw, and nearly lost an ear. I was ashamed of this performance as I had stooped so low in the ring that night as to be partly to blame, for what should have been entertainment ended up being nothing better than a pub brawl, and not the professional standard that was expected of us by our paying audience. I felt bad about that, but not bad enough, obviously, to prevent further outbreaks between us on two further occasions.

Finally, the inevitable happened and we were summoned to head office and brought up in front of the promoters (they did have the sense not to summon us at the same time. We each received a written warning and a reprimand. We were never to appear on the same bill again, which suited us fine, and should there be any further problems, contracts would be terminated.

Thinking back, I suppose I got off lightly, as they could have dropped me totally. If one of us had to go, then it would have been me, as he was one of their biggest attractions and would have been pretty safe. I, on the other hand, in the great scheme of things was just fodder.

As this book is titled *Confessions Of A Wrestler* I would be failing my readers if I didn't admit that some years later, a smirk came to my face when I heard of his death. Not something I feel proud of, but nevertheless true.

There was friction between wrestlers, but thankfully it was quite a rare event and it only happened to me once. Most of those I met were helpful and good people to be around. I couldn't have asked for better workmates.

It takes a lot of people to put on an evening of wrestling and there are plenty of workers in the background who you never see and seldom are at the venues during the show, but without them, the show just wouldn't go on.

One of the key characters in the game in those days was the late and great Kent Walton. In case you don't know, he was the voice of television wrestling. Born in 1917 in Cairo, he lived in Surrey and started off his career as a sports commentator with Radio Luxembourg. He had several similar positions elsewhere before he worked in wrestling.

Kent commentated on the first televised bout way back in 1955, and stayed with it to the very end. The music would play and his first words were, "Greetings, grapple fans" (I can hear him now). He was a good man and a proud man, who used to boast in a good-humoured way that two of the game's biggest fans were Margaret Thatcher and Her Majesty The Queen. He died on the 24th of August 2003, two days after his 86th birthday.

I would also like to pay tribute to the ring riggers. These were the people who would travel around the country erecting the rings and setting out the chairs, hanging the big lighting systems from the ceilings and generally preparing the halls. There were many such gangs on the go at the same time. It was not unusual for some promoters to have five or six venues on the go on any one night. And of course, after the show, they would have to take the ring away, stack the chairs and tidy up before moving on. People never saw these men, but they were the backbone of the industry.

It was a job made even more difficult if it was being filmed, as you then had to do all this work without tripping over cables and other equipment that was in the way.

Also, spare a thought for the bill posters who had to go out in all weather and put up the posters. They walked miles each day with very little reward. I know - I've done it.

Celebrity encounters

By the time I had been wrestling for a few years I was accepted not only by my fellow fighters, but by the paying audiences. I was, I guess you could say, becoming a household name among the wrestling fans and would be recognized by the majority, in certain parts of the country. OK, I was signing my share of autographs in the street and in restaurants, but don't get me wrong, if it was a toss-up between me and Cliff Richard's gardener, I reckon I would have been runner up.

However, the point of this detail is relevant to my next tale. I don't remember the venue but it was somewhere in London, and as I happened to be wrestling some fifteen miles away on the following night, I, with one or two others, decided that what was needed was a boys' night out in the great metropolis.

Naturally, we headed for the most popular area, which at that time was the West End. We visited several places of interest (OK then, pubs) and as all young lads of our age do, we ended up in Soho. I had decided that I was going to visit a well-known club that seemed to specialize in jazz. I have to admit that I was not too enthusiastic about jazz, but it was a better option for me than sticking with my mates and going to see a film in some little seedy back-street room full of cigarette smoke and long macs (need I say more.)

I ordered myself a drink and looked around for a seat; there were quite a few as in clubland, "the night was young." I glanced over to my left and nearly dropped my drink. Sitting at a table was that great and much-loved actor John Le Mesurier, famous not only for his great role as Sergeant Wilson in that icon of comedies Dad's Army, but from many films I had seen.

I stood there for a few minutes plucking up the courage to wander over and say hello. I think it was the realisation that this chance would never come again that finally made me move towards the table - it was either that or I was starstruck - but eventually I introduced myself to him.

"My dear chap, how nice to meet you, pull up a chair and join me, won't you" he said. I could hardly believe my ears, it was as if he'd known me for years. We chatted for a while and I must admit to being mesmerized by his voice, which, as you know, was as soft as petals and perfectly charming.

"Now tell me how you came to get into wrestling, I find it fascinating" he said.

I relayed the story of my early years and how I had slept in a caravan with two strippers and a bearded lady. He gently put his head back and laughed and laughed. "Well that's quite a coincidence," he said. "My wife, dear Joanie, came from a similar background you know, her family were in the circus business." And so it went on. We shared a few laughs and more than a few drinks that night. I finally took my leave, as tiredness had kicked in and the drinks had taken their toll.

We shook hands and with his parting words, "When you fight in London again, let me know and I will be sure to come along, I will hold you to that mind." I returned to my hotel. What a wonderful, friendly man John was. If he had been a stick of rock he would have had "Pure Gentleman" written right through it. Sadly our paths were never to cross again and I was saddened to hear some time later that he had passed away. I still smile to myself whenever I see him in those most welcome re-runs of Dads Army.

It didn't always happen that way though. A while later I was relaxing in a bar one night in Monmouth after a particularly long journey from Newcastle and a very arduous bout of eight five-minute rounds with a fellow wrestler who tipped the scales around the 20-stone mark. As I approached the bar, which was mainly frequented by locals, I caught site of a popular comedian who I had seen many times on the television. I will call him Ben, as I have no wish to cause his family any embarrassment. I nodded to him and said "Hello Ben". He looked me up and down and replied, "Who are you? I don't know you, bugger off."

One of his drinking cronies leaned in towards him and said. "Don't you know who that is? He's a wrestler, been on the telly quite a bit." With that, Ben shouted across the bar, "Do you want a drink mate?" As a person who likes to treat people the way they treat me, I shouted back. "No thanks, I'll buy my own, I'm particular who I drink with, and you can bugger off too." With that, I picked up my drink and sat at a table a few yards away.

Luck was on my side that night as it wasn't long before a small group of lads came over and asked for autographs. I obliged (as I always did) and they sat around and we chatted about wrestling, in particular, my bout that evening, as they had been in the audience.

It wasn't long before Bugger Off Ben's cronies had left him and he was on his own. I glanced in his direction a few times and once or twice caught him looking at me. Although I am not a vindictive person by nature, I really felt that he had had his comeuppance on that occasion. I watched him on television many times after that and I have to say that he always made me laugh and will go down in my book as one of the finest comedians of his day. It was a shame that he was an ignoramus off the stage.

Another encounter I remember was with the great Max Bygraves. (If you are old enough to remember the days of wrestling on the television, you will know the gentleman in question.) He was the king of comedy entertainers many years ago. I had arrived in Bournemouth in plenty of time for my evening fight and was taking a stroll around that lovely seaside resort when I happened to pass a small group of girls who were laughing and giggling, standing around a Rolls Royce. As I came nearer, one of the girls shouted, "There's Jackie Evans coming, Hey Jackie, come and say hello to Max Bygraves." I walked over and said "Hello Max".

"So you're Jackie Evans the wrestler then?" he replied. He didn't know me at all, but one of the girls had obviously tipped him off. He put out his hand and I shook it. "I don't know whether to shake your hand or give you a beating" he joked.

"And I don't know whether to tell you a story." I quickly replied, that being his catchphrase. "Don't be cheeky, laddie" he said through smiling teeth, then thought better of it. He gave me a friendly slap on the back and quickly said, "Don't take it seriously my friend, I'm only joking." I was ready for him. "Max, how can I take a man who sings a song about a couple of flipping toothbrushes seriously?"

We chatted for a few minutes after the girl groupies had dispersed, and then went on our way, him, in his Roller and me on foot.

His last remark was to ask me if I could get him a ticket for the wrestling that evening, as he would like to come along. I agreed to it but was not expecting him to turn up. However, I left word about him on the door and carried on with my business. I was the last bout on that evening and as I was leaving the ring, I caught sight of him sitting towards the back of the hall. I nodded to him as I passed, and he nodded back. By the time I had taken my shower and emerged from the dressing room he had gone. I had hoped that we could have had a drink together afterwards. I was going to tap him up for a couple of free tickets to one of his shows. Never mind, I had at least met him and was able to confirm that he was a thoroughly nice chap.

Another firm favourite from my youth was Leslie Crowther, not just an accomplished comedian of the time but an all-round entertainer. I remember him from *Crackerjack*, which was a popular children's show when I was a lot younger.

I met Leslie in a café in that wonderful city of Bath, and we got talking. Not that he recognized me, it was just that we were the only two in there at the time. We chatted over a cup of coffee and as I remembered, the main subject was about the changes he had witnessed in that great city. He was very passionate about Bath and showed concern in case it should lose its architectural and historic character. He need not have worried, for as far as I can make out, it still retains its splendour. It was a pleasant way to spend an hour and I shall always remember it.

Some years later I heard that he had been involved in a car accident and had been diagnosed with a blood clot on the brain. His health deteriorated as a result and he was to sadly pass away a few years later with heart failure.

That's the problem with recalling memories from years gone by - many of the people have now passed away. Writing this book is giving me a great deal of satisfaction and amusement. It has forced me to remember a great deal that would normally have stayed in that dark cupboard at the back of my brain. It is such a shame that occasionally, it has to be tinged with sadness, but hey, that's life.

The final curtain

As the saying goes "all good things must come to an end", and for me, last orders were called around 1980. There were rumours flying around that wrestling, was going to be taken off of the television. We were not surprised to hear that, as it was evident that it had seen better days and its popularity was suffering.

There were several theories as to why it had lost its sparkle and the most popular was the introduction of those two oversized wrestlers Big Daddy and Giant Haystacks. They were good enough at what they did, but it meant that the wrestling skills that had been on show over the years were giving way to a couple of very large gentlemen belly-butting each other into the canvas. The bouts that I remember featuring those two, rarely lasted more than a few minutes and people were not going to pay good money for so little entertainment. It had little to do with traditional wrestling and more to do with bad showmanship. Whatever the real reason, we all felt that the days of professional wrestling, in its traditional form, were numbered.

I remember having a conversation with two friends who had been in the business a lot longer than me, and we debated whether we should jump or wait to be pushed. The game seemed to be as popular as ever in the halls up and down the country, but eventually the knock-on effect would put paid to that. We chatted into the small hours at an all-night transport café just outside Liverpool. My dilemma seemed to be worse than that of my two mates as they had for some years, been working as actors and were carving themselves a respectable portfolio to that effect.

I gave it some thought but eventually decided against that route. I didn't mind doing acting, but as the saying goes, I didn't want to give up the day job. No, I would find myself a steady job, even if it meant going back to college and re-training.

As we left and said goodbye, I wondered if they would be as popular as actors as they had been as wrestlers. I needn't have worried as they both proved their worth in their new-found work. One was my mate of many years, Pat Roach, who I have mentioned already. In addition to his role in *Auf Wiedersehen Pet* he appeared in James Bond films and much more besides. Pat also had great success with a gymnasium which he owned and ran in Birmingham.

The other man was a wrestler who was known in the ring as Leon Aris but is probably better remembered as Brian Glover. Brian proved to have an exceptional talent for acting and went on to fame and success, delivering some amazing performances. The first role of his I recall was as the PE teacher in a lovely Yorkshire-based film called *Kes*, about a young lad who befriends a kestrel and learns to fly the bird and have it come back to him. Brian also appeared in voice-overs on many adverts which needed a broad Yorkshire accent, and he played a popular character in the television series *Porridge* alongside the great Ronnie Barker. So versatile was he that I saw him in many parts over the years, and I even saw him on television playing Shakespeare. Two most wonderful actors who, I must say, have made my life richer for knowing them both.

For my own part, I went back to college and finally, university, and took up my present profession of specializing in physical injuries, which have afforded me a good living over the years. It seemed a fitting thing to do - my early years consisted of bending muscles and bones about so it seemed natural that I should spend my later years repairing them. I have worked in and owned several surgeries over the years and now I tend to work from home, which is a lot easier to manage as I am under threat of castration from some patients if I ever retire from the business. I took up several hobbies as well, ones I had always meant to do throughout the years but never got around to it.

Amateur dramatics was one of them. It is still something I am involved with today, although I do not go on the stage much now, as I am too old to remember the lines. As I am a keen DIY enthusiast, I get to make up props and bits of furniture for the group I am with. Any spare time I have I spend in the garden, where I can work at my own pace and remember the active times throughout my life whilst trying to keep the old bones active.

I think, looking back, that I made the right decision at the time. It was five more years before television wrestling was finally taken off, but my strategy was to quit while I was ahead.

Did I make it to the top? Well - who can say? Like the famous five in African animal terms, there were five top wrestlers in my day: Mick McManus, Jackie Pallo, Steve Logan, Les Kellett and of course, the finest, skilled wrestler of them all, George Kidd. Was I up among them? Of course I wasn't. What about the next line up, Adrian Street, Bert Royal, Vic Faulkner, Pat Roach, and many more besides? Hmm - debatable. It doesn't really matter. The fact that I was among them and friends with them, and had a damn good time while making a living is enough for me. I wouldn't have missed it for the world, and if I had my time over again, I wouldn't change a thing.

It was hard work, especially with the amount of travelling involved, but what an experience. It has left me with many fond memories of the whole business. To think that I should end up in the ring, working with the same people who had been my childhood idols, fills me with a sense of achievement and pride.

When I meet people nowadays and they get to know me, it is invariably my time in the wrestling game that they want to talk about. Had I met Mick Mc Manus? Did I ever wrestle Jackie Pallo? They are also keen to tell me of their experiences as members of the audience, which is always good to hear.

I must say that even after all these years, I can still get my old wrestling boots on. I only wish I could get down to tie the damn things up. I have to confess that I never watch the American-style of wrestling that is popular now. I tried to watch it once, but felt that it lacked that sparkle that was there in the seventies. I'm sure it's very good, but it's not for me. I'm glad I did it, but I'm also glad I stopped when the time came.

I did wrestle once more, about a year later. I was taking a family holiday at Butlins, and of course, gravitated to the wrestling that was on show there. It was a bit sad really, as I patted the ring on the way in like I was greeting an old friend. There were to be two bouts as was the usual.

I noticed that there was something wrong when the first bout was still going on after nearly an hour. No one seemed to notice except me, so off I went to find the promoter. It was as I had thought - the second bout wrestlers had not yet turned up. I knew the promoter from several years before and it didn't take much persuading for me to step in and challenge the dirtiest wrestler to a fight. Luckily, it was one of my old mates Maurice from Bristol. I leapt up onto the ringside and wagged my finger at him, shouting that I would challenge him. Of course, the crowd was with me. He was surprised to see me at first, but then realising what was happening he accepted the challenge. Back in the changing rooms, they quickly found me some tools (wrestling gear) and that was how I found myself back in the ring.

However, it was short lived. Having been out of the game for a year, I was wrestling like a sack of potatoes, and boy, was I out of condition. Good old Maurice did his best to help me through five long, agonizing rounds, but eventually he beat me by two submissions to one. The crowd had enjoyed it, the promoter was grateful and I was knackered. I did have a long chat to some old buddies, which made it all worthwhile, but that was my last and final throw of the dice. From that day to this, I have never been back inside a ring, and I don't think I ever will.

I did, however, meet up with a few of them from time to time, and my old friend Pat Roach came down to open a health and fitness exhibition in my now local town of Andover in Hampshire. By then he was a well-known actor, so he helped to draw in the crowds. It was good to see him after several years as we reminisced about the good old days.

It was a sad time when both Brian Glover and Pat Roach passed away in their sixties, Brian in 1997 from a brain tumour and Pat in 2004 from cancer. The world had lost two brilliant actors and wrestlers and I had lost two good mates. But I haven't completely lost them, they are still here, in my head, and always will be. Nobody can ever take that away from me.

I do have one slight regret. A few years ago, I was

clearing out an old shed at home when I happened to come across some old wrestling bits and pieces, among them about 15 hair bows from Jackie Pallo. He used to wear them into the ring and throw them to the crowd. They were neat little things, black with "Jackie Mr TV Pallo" on them in gold. I put them on the bonfire and thought no more about it until a few years later when Jackie sadly died. Someone told me they were fetching up to £150 on ebay. I could have cried. Never mind, at least I had the pleasure of meeting the man himself.

I would also like to mention here all the millions of wrestling fans who, through their dedication and interest in the game, made it possible for people like me to live their dream. Without them, the game would have been lost before it had even begun. Not only those who followed it every Saturday on the television but those who would trudge to their local halls, in all weathers, to give us their support. We could not have done it without you.

In fact, I would like to pay tribute to all the wrestlers that I was proud to know, those who are still with us and those who have gone, and to all the other people who made the game what it was and have contributed to what has now become, and will always be, the golden age of wrestling. It is a shame it has now been consigned to the history books, but heartening to see that there are many websites on the internet dedicated to the good old days when professional wrestling was a cult. Wrestling may not be what it was (although I believe it still goes on in some halls up and down the country and in some holiday camps), but thanks to those enthusiastic diehards, it will never be forgotten. For my part, I still find people who want to talk about those days, and I for one am happy to do so. I hope that you find as much enjoyment in reading this book as I have in writing it.

As time goes on, I find myself being told that I do not look like a wrestler - but hey, when I was a lad that old chap in front of me at the bus stop didn't look the sort who would parachute into enemy territory. And that dear old wife of his doesn't resemble the lovely girl who once drove an ambulance through the streets of London during an air raid. Life doesn't stop at our finest hour, it goes on.

I was reminded of this a couple of weeks ago when I sadly attended the funeral of my old friend Reg Ball, better known as Reg Presley, lead singer of the 1960s pop group The Troggs. A funeral is always a sad occasion, but this was made more poignant by the sheer number of mourners. It was like a 1960s pop convention, but instead of guitars and microphones there were walking sticks, zimmer frames and wheelchairs. No one could doubt the sheer talent that was there among us, people who had not only shaped the world of music into what it is today but had shaped many of our lives in that age-old art of growing up. They had certainly played a part in my life, albeit a small one. I like to think that my time in the ring had played a role in people's lives, maybe not a significant one, but nevertheless, a role. Nothing earth-shattering of course, just a bit of entertainment for the odd hour now and then. That thought helps to compensate for the depression that tends to set in when you are forced to accept that the young virile fighter showing his talent and youthfulness in front of you on the television is, in fact yourself. Not a comforting thought as you reach for your slippers and pick up your Horlicks of an evening.

Those of us who are fit enough to travel meet up at least once a year at the great wrestlers' reunion, held, very kindly by Wayne Bridges and his lovely wife Sarah in their most welcoming pub in Kent. The event is put together by Wayne and Sarah with the help of two other icons from those golden days, Frank Rimer and Joe D'Orazio. It is a great day out and a chance to chat to some memorable friends from my younger days, such as Johnny Kincaid, Mal Sanders, Steve Grey and many more besides. There are no longer the good guys and the bad guys, those days are gone. To me, each and every one of them is the salt of the earth. Long may they continue as I pay my respects to them all.

Printed in Great Britain
by Amazon

42526481R00145